# TORN

## LIVING ON EARTH WHILE LONGING FOR HEAVEN

DR. BRUCE BECKER

Published by Straight Talk Books
P.O. Box 301, Milwaukee, WI 53201
800.661.3311 • timeofgrace.org



Printed in the United States of America

ISBN: 978-1-965694-11-4

# CONTENTS

# INTRODUCTION

I started writing this book in the spring of 2020. It was originally sketched out to be a book about how Old and New Testament believers lived as exiles in their respective cultures as well as how Christians today live as exiles in our current culture. Although I had a good start on the book, I didn't feel good about where the book was going. It was too generic, too bland, too boring. So it found its way to the circular file.

Strike one.

At the encouragement of a few of my colleagues, I didn't give up on the book. I took a second swing at it. This time I added tons of detail about events that were playing out in the culture during the last decade. Those events revealed how Christians are truly living as outsiders in our culture, living in exile. Our Time of Grace team had scheduled the book to be published in April 2023. But upon reading the manuscript, a few of my colleagues thought it was too descriptive and a bit too controversial. I respect their perspective. Other colleagues thought that the book tackled some tough cultural topics in an objective and helpful way. Split decision. In the end, it was decided not to publish it, at least not as it was written.

Strike two.

Several months later, in the summer of 2023, our family vacationed in the mountains of Utah, northeast of Salt Lake City. During that weeklong time together, I had several opportunities to chat with members of my family about the book, its challenges, and its back-burner status. I figured I needed some outside perspective.

My wife, Linda, encouraged me to continue to work on the book because of all the research and work that I had already put into it. My three adult kids—Christopher, Andrew, and Deanna (who are all millennials)—suggested that Christians today really need to think through both the *challenges* and *opportunities* that followers of Jesus have living as exiles in our current culture. The consensus among the three was, "Dad, we need a book about Christians living and serving in our current culture." They encouraged me to take another swing at it along with several of my colleagues at Time of Grace.

Swing!

The fact that you are reading this book means I didn't strike out. Whew!

Just as there were multiple drafts of this book, so also there were multiple working titles, each conveying the nuances of each draft. After outlining the third draft of this book, my son Chris suggested a title—*Torn*. I liked his title because it captured the essence of this book. But even more so, it captured the spirit of what the apostle Paul wrote in his letter to the Christians living in Philippi, a spirit that exists among all believers of all time:

> **Yes, and I will continue to rejoice, for I know that through your prayers and God's provision of the Spirit of Jesus Christ what has happened to me will turn out for my deliverance. I eagerly expect and hope that I will in no way be ashamed, but will have sufficient courage so that now as always Christ will be exalted in my body, whether by life or by death. For to me, to live is Christ and to die is gain. If I am to go on living in the body, this will mean fruitful labor for me. Yet what shall I choose? I do not know! I am torn between the two: I desire to depart and be with Christ, which is better by far; but it is more necessary for you that I remain in the body. Convinced of this, I know that I will remain, and I will continue with all of you for your progress and joy in the faith, so that through my being with you again your boasting in Christ Jesus will abound on account of me.** (Philippians 1:18-26)

To appreciate fully what Paul wrote here, we need to remember that Paul wrote this letter while he was in prison in Rome. Now to be clear, Paul wasn't locked up in some damp, dark, and dusty dungeon. He actually lived in a rented house along with a Roman soldier who was stationed there to guard him. In other words, Paul was under house arrest, which meant that although he was a prisoner, he could continue his calling of proclaiming the good news about Jesus.

But how did Paul end up under house arrest in the first place? After Paul had completed his third missionary journey, he returned to Jerusalem. He met with the leaders of the church in Jerusalem and shared all the amazing things that the Lord God had done through his missionary work among the Gentiles in Asia and Europe.

Shortly after his return to Jerusalem, a group of Jews from Asia spotted him and accused him of teaching contrary to Jewish law and defiling the temple by allowing Gentiles to step foot in it. These Jewish leaders stirred up the entire city, which resulted in an angry mob attempting to kill Paul. Their murderous plan was squelched when Roman soldiers showed up and took Paul into custody.

Long story short, Paul was taken to Caesarea, where he endured three different trials over the course of several years. Each one of these trials was without merit. All three trials were 1st-century versions of 21st-century "lawfare." "Lawfare" is when people use the legal systems and institutions to damage or undermine an opponent. In the final trial before King Agrippa, it became clear that the Jewish leaders would never be satisfied with anything short of Paul's death. So Paul, as a Roman citizen, made a last-ditch effort to avoid being murdered. He appealed to Caesar.

By appealing to Caesar, Paul could escape from those who wanted him dead. He was sent to Rome to stand trial before Caesar. There was a second reason that Paul wanted to get to Rome. Prior to a previous second attempt on Paul's life by the Jewish mob, Jesus told Paul that he would be going to Rome. We read in the book of Acts: **"The following night the Lord stood near Paul and said, 'Take courage! As you have testified about me in Jerusalem, so you must also testify in Rome'"** (23:11). Paul's journey to Rome was part of God's plan. It was part of God's plan for his church.

Bible scholars suggest that Paul's imprisonment in Rome occurred between A.D. 60 and 62. Even though he was only under house arrest awaiting trial, Paul didn't know his future fate. Would he spend the rest of his life as a prisoner? Would he be executed? Or would he be released one day? Paul's uncertainty about his future was unmasked in what he wrote to the Christians living in Philippi: *"I am torn between the two."* Paul was torn. He was torn between departing this world to live with Christ for all eternity ("which is better by far"!) and between remaining as an exile in this world to proclaim Jesus and to serve and love people.

The phrase translated as "I am torn between the two" is a complex idiom. My favorite Greek lexicon explains it this way: "to be in a mental state between two alternatives—'to be pulled in two directions, to be betwixt and between, to have conflicting thoughts.' . . . In a number of languages the rendering of this statement in Php 1:23 must be expressed idiomatically, for example, 'my mind is pulling me in two directions' or 'my thoughts are going in two different directions' or 'my heart is speaking two different words to me.'"[1] The apostle Paul was pulled in two different directions. He was torn.

We're torn too.

We're torn on multiple levels. Like the apostle Paul, we're torn between wanting to be home with Jesus and fulfilling the calling that our God has given us here on this earth. In other words, we're torn between a personal preference (heaven) and a personal calling (earth). We're also torn because we're living as exiles in our culture (more on this in the next chapter), torn between living in the culture while not being of the culture. Finally, we feel torn because our *faith* is being attacked with the *fear* generated by the culture. Our *hope* is being undermined by the *despair* all around us. And our *love* is under constant threat because of the *hate* that permeates our culture. All these factors contribute to you and me living torn lives.

In chapter 1, we'll explore what it means to live as exiles while living in this world. Then in the succeeding chapters, we'll explore examples of how God's people, in both the Old and New Testaments, lived as exiles in their respective cultures. More important, we'll learn from them how to navigate our culture and how to be a positive influence in our culture. Two themes that are threaded throughout this book are *challenges* and *opportunities*. Living as an exile has its challenges. But it also has its opportunities. These two themes contribute to us living our lives torn.

All God's people, from the beginning of this world until the end of it, will have lived their lives as exiles in this world.

God's people have always lived their lives *torn*.

# CHAPTER 1

# LIVING IN EXILE WHILE LIVING IN THE WORLD

## EARLY A.D. 60S

*Dear friends,*

*I urge you, as foreigners and exiles, to abstain from sinful desires, which wage war against your soul. Live such good lives among the pagans that, though they accuse you of doing wrong, they may see your good deeds and glorify God on the day he visits us.* (1 Peter 2:11,12)

**In Christ's love,**

**Peter**

Do you know anyone personally who has had to live in exile due to political, social, or economic circumstances? Maybe not personally, but perhaps you've heard of such people in a high school history class or read about their lives in biographical sketches or stumbled across their stories online. Did you know that throughout history, countless people have been forced to live in exile, including hundreds of kings and queens, emperors, sultans, presidents, and monarchs? These sovereign rulers were forced into exile by others who, at the time, had greater power and influence than they did.

One such emperor whom I recall from a college history course was Napoleon Bonaparte. He was a unique monarch in that he was exiled twice in his life. Napoleon was just one of several hundred monarchs in history who were forced to live in exile.

A more recent example of an exiled head of state is Ashraf Ghani, the former president of Afghanistan. His exile began in August 2021 when the Taliban deposed him and overthrew his government. It occurred just days after the U.S. military left his country.

Although countless people, not just heads of state, have been forced to live in exile, there are many more individuals who have *chosen* to live in exile. The reasons why people choose self-exile vary greatly.

Some choose to live in exile to escape persecution in their homelands. For example, during World War II, many Jewish people fled Germany to escape Hitler's plan to carry out genocide against them. Or you may recall the many Cuban citizens—more than a million—who have fled their island home. This exodus began with the Cuban Revolution in the 1950s and continues yet today.

Others choose to live in exile because of legal or tax reasons. One example, apparently for economic reasons, was Eduardo Saverin. Saverin was one of the founders of Facebook. Prior to the company's initial public offering, Saverin fled to Singapore and in 2011 renounced his U.S. citizenship. Although he claims to have moved to Singapore for more noble reasons, he did save himself an estimated $700 million in capital gains taxes by leaving the U.S.

Still others have chosen to live in exile because of the crimes they have committed in their home countries. In the past year, I recall reading about a California man who had been convicted of fraud and tax evasion in December 2000. His name was Robin McPherson. Instead of showing up for his sentencing hearing, McPherson skipped town and headed to Costa Rica, where he lived in exile for more than two decades. The U.S. FBI and Costa Rican authorities worked together to find him, arrest him, and bring him back to face his crimes. His exile in Costa Rica has ended. McPherson is currently living in another kind of exile.

In the history of the world, there have been many individuals exiled against their will. In other cases, individuals have chosen to live in exile for a variety of reasons. But did you know that there is a third group of people in another category of exile? It's a group of people who aren't *forced* to live in exile, nor do they *choose* to live in exile. They just *are* in exile.

I'm talking about you and me.

In both of the New Testament letters penned by the apostle Peter, he wrote to first-century Christ followers scattered across the Roman Empire. He began his first letter:

> **Peter, an apostle of Jesus Christ,**
>
> **To God's elect, exiles scattered throughout the provinces of Pontus, Galatia, Cappadocia, Asia and Bithynia, who have been chosen according to the foreknowledge of God the Father, through the sanctifying work of the Spirit, to be obedient to Jesus Christ and sprinkled with his blood:**
>
> **Grace and peace be yours in abundance.**
> (1 Peter 1:1,2)

Then in 1 Peter chapter 2, Peter again referred to the recipients of his letter as *foreigners* and *exiles*. The two Greek words that Peter used in his original letter are quite similar in meaning. To live as a foreigner or in exile means living for a period of time in a place that is not a person's normal place of residence.

Kind of like snowbirds. A snowbird is a person who travels to warmer climates typically for the months of January, February, and/or March. They go to escape the snow and cold of the northern continental climates. They are people who live for a period of time in a place that is not their normal residence. States like Arizona, Florida, Texas, New Mexico, and others have their own flocks of snowbirds.

Unlike snowbirds though, these first-century Christ

followers became exiles because of persecution. This persecution was real, and it was severe. Many lost their lives because they followed Jesus.

In Acts chapter 7, we learn about the first Christian martyr. His name was Stephen. He was stoned to death because of his testimony about Jesus in his speech to the Sanhedrin, the Jewish ruling council. Then we read what happened on the day of Stephen's death:

> **On that day a great persecution broke out against the church in Jerusalem, and all except the apostles were scattered throughout Judea and Samaria. Godly men buried Stephen and mourned deeply for him. But Saul began to destroy the church. Going from house to house, he dragged off both men and women and put them in prison.** (Acts 8:1–3)

In *some* cases, these first-century Christians were living in exile because they had to flee their homeland to escape persecution. In *every* case, however, these followers of Christ lived in exile in a different sense. It was the type of exile that Jesus talked about shortly before his death.

In John chapter 17, Jesus prayed to his heavenly Father. This prayer has been called Jesus' High Priestly Prayer. That's because in this prayer, Jesus served as the High Priest, who interceded before his heavenly Father on behalf of his disciples and all believers, you and me included. Let's listen in on a section of Jesus' prayer for his followers:

"I have revealed you to those whom you gave me out of the world. They were yours; you gave them to me and they have obeyed your word. Now they know that everything you have given me comes from you. For I gave them the words you gave me and they accepted them. They knew with certainty that I came from you, and they believed that you sent me. I pray for them. I am not praying for the world, but for those you have given me, for they are yours. All I have is yours, and all you have is mine. And glory has come to me through them. I will remain in the world no longer, but *they are still in the world*, and I am coming to you. Holy Father, protect them by the power of your name, the name you gave me, so that they may be one as we are one. While I was with them, I protected them and kept them safe by that name you gave me. None has been lost except the one doomed to destruction so that Scripture would be fulfilled.

"I am coming to you now, but I say these things while I am still in the world, so that they may have the full measure of my joy within them. *I have given them your word and the world has hated them, for they are not of the world any more than I am of the world.* My prayer is not that you take them out of the world but that you protect them from the evil one. *They are not of the world, even as I am not of it.* Sanctify

> **them by the truth; your word is truth. As you sent me into the world, I have sent them into the world. For them I sanctify myself, that they too may be truly sanctified.**
>
> **"My prayer is not for them alone. I pray also for those who will believe in me through their message, that all of them may be one, Father, just as you are in me and I am in you. May they also be in us so that the world may believe that you have sent me."** (verses 6–21, emphasis added)

In this section of John's gospel, the phrases in italics are key to understanding this unique kind of exile that all first-century Christ followers experienced. Although Jesus returned to his heavenly Father, his followers remained *in* the world. Even though his followers were *in* the world, they were not *of* the world any more than Jesus was *of* the world. What's the distinction?

First-century followers of Jesus were physically present in the world but no longer part of its culture, values, morals, norms, and priorities. When they became followers of Jesus, a monumental change took place in their lives. When the Holy Spirit, through the power of the gospel, created faith in their hearts, they were transformed from living in the darkness of sin and unbelief to living in the light and life of Jesus. We call this personal transformation "conversion."

Conversion resulted in those first Christians no longer being *of* the world, only *in* the world. Conversion resulted in living their new lives in exile, as foreigners or strangers, because following Christ is *counter* to the *culture*. In *Merriam-Webster*'s online entry for the word *counterculture*, it says it's "a culture with values and mores that run counter to those of established society." Those first-century Christians lived counter to the culture. They lived with faith in the face of fear, with hope in the midst of despair, and with love when surrounded by hate.

Conversion also required those first-century Christ followers to navigate the culture in which they still lived, a culture that was openly hostile to them. However, living as exiles didn't mean they retreated from the culture or crawled into a culture-safe bunker. It also didn't mean that they became cynics or spent all their time whining about the culture. Just the opposite.

What was true for those first-century believers is also true of us. As followers of Christ, we seek to be positive and influential in our culture, letting our light shine, doing good, serving others, and pointing people to what matters most: Jesus. When it comes to living in exile, we need to think actively, not passively. We may live counter to the culture, but we seek to affect the culture in a positive way.

The 19th-century English songwriter Thomas Rawson Taylor captured this concept of living in exile while living in the world. It was a hymn he wrote during a serious illness he experienced shortly before his death. The year was 1835.

I've heard and sung this hymn dozens, if not hundreds, of times and almost always at funerals. It's a hymn that captures the fact that as followers of Christ, we live in this world as aliens, exiles, and strangers:

**Stanza 1**

*I'm but a stranger here;*
*Heaven is my home.*
*Earth is a desert drear;*
*Heaven is my home.*
*Danger and sorrow stand*
*Round me on every hand.*
*Heaven is my fatherland;*
*Heaven is my home.*

**Stanza 2**

*What though the tempest rage,*
*Heaven is my home.*
*Short is my pilgrimage;*
*Heaven is my home.*
*And time's wild, wintry blast*
*Soon shall be overpast;*
*I shall reach home at last;*
*Heaven is my home.*

**Stanza 3**

*There at my Savior's side*
*Heaven is my home—*
*I shall be glorified;*
*Heaven is my home.*
*There are the good and blest,*
*Those I love most and best,*
*And there I, too, shall rest;*
*Heaven is my home.*

**Stanza 4**

*Therefore I murmur not;*
*Heaven is my home.*
*Whate'er my earthly lot,*
*Heaven is my home.*
*And I shall surely stand*
*There at my Lord's right hand.*
*Heaven is my fatherland;*
*Heaven is my home.*[2]

We're living in exile while living in the world. And because we're living as exiles, we live our lives torn, torn between wanting to be with our Creator and Savior and living our lives as God's people, giving him glory, pointing people to Jesus, and serving others in love.

But living in exile is nothing new. It's been true since the days of Noah.

# CHAPTER 2

# NOAH

The account of Noah begins halfway through Genesis chapter 6. However, before we get to Noah and the culture in which he lived, let's review and summarize the content of the previous five chapters of Genesis. This will set the stage for the cultural context in the days of Noah.

Genesis chapters 1 and 2 detail the creation of the universe, including the creation of the first man and the first woman, Adam and Eve. One of the unique and special aspects of their creation was that they were created in God's image.

Genesis chapter 3 features the sad story of how the serpent Satan tempted the first couple and led them to disobey God's one command, the command not to eat the fruit of the tree of the knowledge of good and evil. This one act destroyed the relationship between the Creator and his creation. Fortunately for us, God didn't abandon his creation but promised Adam and Eve a rescue plan that would restore their relationship.

Chapter 4 records the murder of Abel by his brother Cain and the sad consequences of that crime, consequences that lasted for many centuries. Cain's murder of his brother Abel initiated the evil that would explode in the world until the time of Noah.

Chapter 5 chronicles Adam's descendants until the time of Noah. One striking detail about this list of descendants is how many years many of them lived on the earth before they died. We also learn about one of Adam's descendants, a man by the name of Enoch: **"Altogether, Enoch lived a total of 365 years. Enoch walked faithfully with God; then he was no more, because God took him away"** (Genesis 5:23,24). Enoch was one of two people in the Old Testament who did not face natural death (although there is nothing "natural" about death from God's original design). The other was Elijah the prophet. This chapter also gives us a sense of how many centuries elapsed from Adam to Noah.

This brings us to Genesis chapter 6. The first eight verses of this chapter describe the culture at Noah's time. Let's start with the first four verses:

> **When human beings began to increase in number on the earth and daughters were born to them, the sons of God saw that the daughters of humans were beautiful, and they married any of them they chose. Then the LORD said, "My Spirit will not contend with humans forever, for they are mortal; their days will be a hundred and twenty years."**
>
> **The Nephilim were on the earth in those days—and**

> **also afterward—when the sons of God went to the daughters of humans and had children by them. They were the heroes of old, men of renown.**

After reading these verses, a few questions come to mind. Who were the sons of God? Who were the daughters of men? And who in the world were the Nephilim?

In October 2025, Time of Grace is planning to publish another book that I authored. The book was originally a podcast series by the name *War Zone* that was published on my podcast, *Bible Threads With Dr. Bruce Becker*. In the book and on the podcast, there is a chapter/podcast episode that addresses this section of Genesis chapter 6. The chapter goes into detail about who the sons of God and daughters of humans were as well as who the Nephilim were. In addition, there is an interesting Bible thread that links Genesis chapter 6 with the apostle Peter's two letters and Jude's letter in the New Testament. These three New Testament letters shed light on Genesis chapter 6. We'll be digging into these three letters in chapter 10 of this book.

If you are interested, you can listen to the explanation of Genesis chapter 6 on my podcast (*Bible Threads With Dr. Bruce Becker: War Zone*, Episode 3), or you can read the edited transcript of the podcast in the Appendix of this book (page 203).

For our purposes, we want to focus on the additional details found in these verses. First, we want to focus on the fact that the population of the earth had increased dramatically. We have no idea how many people were living at the time of Noah. Some have estimated that there were as few as 750,000 citizens of Earth. Others have suggested that there were as many as 17 billion. Yes, billion with a *b*. The fact is, however, that we don't know the number, only that the population had increased significantly.

The second takeaway from these verses is that the world had become an evil place. The Lord (that is, Yahweh) indicated that he would not put up with these wicked people indefinitely. Yahweh indicated that their time of grace would be 120 years. And why wouldn't Yahweh put up with them any longer? "For they are mortal; their days will be a hundred and twenty years." The word translated as "mortal" is another way of saying that they were humans with human characteristics and human flaws. The author contrasted the Spirit, who is holy, with humans who are often unholy, evil, and wicked.

The next four verses of Genesis chapter 6 give us some additional insight into the culture of Noah's day:

> **The Lord saw how great the wickedness of the human race had become on the earth, and that every inclination of the thoughts of the human heart was only evil all the time. The Lord regretted that he had made human beings on the earth, and his heart was deeply troubled. So the Lord said, "I will wipe from the face of the earth the human race I have created—and with them the animals, the birds and the creatures that move along the ground—for**

**I regret that I have made them." But Noah found favor in the eyes of the Lord.** (verses 5–8)

Not only was there great wickedness in the world; the author indicates from where that wickedness originated. This is an important point. Yahweh saw not only their outward evil actions; he could also read their hearts. Yahweh observed that "every inclination of the thoughts of the human heart was only evil all the time."

First, let's understand the significance of the two words that describe how ungodly the world had become. Moses, the Spirit-inspired author of the book of Genesis, uses two different Hebrew words that are translated differently in English—"wickedness" and "evil."

The word translated as "wickedness" occurs over one hundred times in the Old Testament. The word has a broad range of meanings. It can refer to evil, misery, and distress. It can also be used to describe injury, harm, and wrongdoing. It can also refer to mischief. The word is often used to describe the injury that the enemies of God's people brought upon God's people. Or it is used in the Old Testament for the kind of disaster that God brought upon his own people when they were unfaithful.

An example of the latter kind of disaster comes from the book of the prophet Isaiah. In these verses, Isaiah describes the misery and distress that would come upon God's people because of their unfaithfulness: **"Disaster will come upon you, and you will not know how to conjure it away. A**

**calamity will fall upon you that you cannot ward off with a ransom; a catastrophe you cannot foresee will suddenly come upon you"** (47:11). Because of their unfaithfulness, God's people would face disaster.

The word translated as "evil" focuses more on the intentions of wickedness. This Hebrew word also occurs more than one hundred times in the Old Testament. It refers more to attitudes that are *bad* as opposed to *good.* These include being disagreeable, inflicting pain, causing misery, being vicious, and causing sadness or unhappiness. Again, a wide range of meanings.

An example of this comes from the book of Esther. (We'll examine the life and culture at the time of Esther in chapter 8.) In Esther, a man named Haman and his sons had devised a plan that would result in the genocide of the Jews. That plan was thwarted after Esther courageously informed the king of Haman's plan: **"But when the plot came to the king's attention, he issued written orders that the evil scheme Haman had devised against the Jews should come back onto his own head, and that he and his sons should be impaled on poles"** (9:25). Yikes! Hardly a humane form of capital punishment, don't you think?

Back to Yahweh's observation: **"Every inclination of the thoughts of the human heart was only evil all the time"** (Genesis 6:5). This description makes the point of the severity and scope of wickedness and evil in the world—"*every* inclination," "*only* evil," and "*all the time.*" The human heart is inclined toward everything wicked and evil.

There is a mirror image of Yahweh's observation in the Old Testament with something Jesus said in the New Testament. Recall what Jesus said when he and his disciples were accused of sin because they ate food without first ceremonially washing their hands. Jesus countered the accusation: **"*For out of the heart* come evil thoughts—murder, adultery, sexual immorality, theft, false testimony, slander. These are what defile a person; but eating with unwashed hands does not defile them"** (Matthew 15:19,20, emphasis added). What defiles a person is what comes out of that person's heart. True in Noah's day. True in Jesus' day. True in our day.

As a result of how wicked the world had become in Noah's day, **"the Lord regretted that he had made human beings on the earth, and his heart was deeply troubled"** (Genesis 6:6). With these words, Moses personified Yahweh in human terms: thinking and using emotions with which we can relate. Yahweh "regretted making humans." In other words, he was "grieved" or "sorry" for how mankind had turned out. This wasn't God's original plan for those whom he had made in his own image. Because of the wickedness in the world, his heart was filled with pain and regret.

Yahweh determined that he had to start over. But why? Two reasons come to mind. First, if Yahweh allowed the wickedness to continue, perhaps all those who were still faithful (and there were likely more than just Noah and his family who were faithful) would eventually fall away as well. A second reason was that if the faithful all fell away, it would break the bloodline thread of the Messiah, the Christ.

You see, in Genesis chapter 3, Yahweh had promised to send a Messiah, a Savior. The Messiah would come through Adam and Eve's descendants. Yet it would be thousands of years before the Messiah would arrive. If there weren't any people faithful to Yahweh remaining on the planet, from whom would the Messiah come? How would God's promise be fulfilled?

So what was Yahweh's reset plan? **"The Lord said, 'I will wipe from the face of the earth the human race I have created—and with them the animals, the birds and the creatures that move along the ground—for I regret that I have made them'"** (Genesis 6:7).

There's something interesting about this reset plan. The Hebrew name for God (translated in English as "God") at creation was Elohim. Elohim is the plural name for God (think Trinity—Father, Son, and Spirit) and emphasizes God's power. On the other hand, Yahweh was the name of the Israelites' God that distinguished Yahweh from other gods like Baal, Asherah, and Molech. The name Yahweh emphasizes God's grace.

Do you recall when God appeared to Moses in a burning bush? God was calling Moses to return to Egypt from his 40-year stay in Midian to lead God's people out of Egypt. During that exchange, **"God said to Moses, 'I am who I am. This is what you are to say to the Israelites: "I am has sent me to you."' God also said to Moses, 'Say to the Israelites, "The Lord, the God of your fathers—the God of Abraham, the God of Isaac and the God of Jacob—has sent me to you"'"**

(Exodus 3:14,15). In these verses, the word translated as "God" in English is "Elohim" in Hebrew. The word translated as "the LORD" in English is "Yahweh" in Hebrew. Two names for the one true God. In the Old Testament, when both names are used together—Yahweh Elohim—they are translated into English as Lord God.

Back to the reset plan. It was Yahweh, the God of grace, who designed this reset plan (even though Yahweh and Elohim are one in the same). Remember, the name Yahweh emphasizes his grace. It was a plan to ensure that his promise to send a Savior to restore the relationship between God and mankind would indeed happen.

In the next verses of Genesis chapter 6, God explains how he would carry out his reset plan along with some additional details about the culture in Noah's day. Note that in this section the name used for God is Elohim, used to emphasize his almighty power:

**This is the account of Noah and his family.**

**Noah was a righteous man, blameless among the people of his time, and he walked faithfully with God. Noah had three sons: Shem, Ham and Japheth.**

**Now the earth was corrupt in God's sight and was full of violence. God saw how corrupt the earth had become, for all the people on earth had corrupted their ways. So God said to Noah, "I am going to put**

**an end to all people, for the earth is filled with violence because of them. I am surely going to destroy both them and the earth."** (verses 9–13)

In contrast to the wickedness and evil in the culture, we meet Noah. He was a righteous man and walked faithfully with God. He was a man of integrity. He was honest. People could trust him. Noah stood in sharp contrast with the majority of people within his culture. Noah lived counter to his culture. Noah was the one whom God chose to be a part of his reset plan.

We learn in these verses about two other cultural realities that existed at the time of Noah. The earth was corrupt, and it was full of violence. The word translated as "corrupt" describes the earth, from God's perspective, as being ruined. The word translated as "violence" is used in the Old Testament to refer to either physical violence, harsh treatment, verbal assaults, or ruthlessness. Violence can be thought of from one of two perspectives, either from the perspective of the one doing the violence or from the one suffering from the violence. From God's perspective, the earth he created was ruined and filled with rampant violence among the people.

So, the Lord God shared his reset plan with Noah:

**"So make yourself an ark of cypress wood; make rooms in it and coat it with pitch inside and out. This is how you are to build it: The ark is to be three hundred cubits long, fifty cubits wide and thirty**

**cubits high. Make a roof for it, leaving below the roof an opening one cubit high all around. Put a door in the side of the ark and make lower, middle and upper decks. I am going to bring floodwaters on the earth to destroy all life under the heavens, every creature that has the breath of life in it. Everything on earth will perish. But I will establish my covenant with you, and you will enter the ark—you and your sons and your wife and your sons' wives with you. You are to bring into the ark two of all living creatures, male and female, to keep them alive with you. Two of every kind of bird, of every kind of animal and of every kind of creature that moves along the ground will come to you to be kept alive. You are to take every kind of food that is to be eaten and store it away as food for you and for them."** (Genesis 6:14-21)

The Lord God instructed Noah to build an ark, a vessel, approximately 450 feet long, 75 feet wide, and 45 feet high. Incredibly, the storage capacity of the vessel would have been 1.5 million cubic feet. The purpose of this vessel was to be a floating zoo and a place of safety for Noah and his family when the Lord God would send a worldwide flood.

Have you ever heard about Noah being mocked or ridiculed for building the ark? I have. Maybe it was in Sunday school or maybe in a sermon I heard as a kid. But do you know what? The Bible never says that Noah was mocked or ridiculed. Knowing the proclivity of our own sinful human nature, it wouldn't be surprising if he was treated with scorn and derision. But that's an assumption we probably shouldn't make because, again, the Bible doesn't say anything about the reaction of Noah's neighbors.

So what else do we know about Noah? Besides the book of Genesis, there are four places in the New Testament that shed additional light on Noah and the culture in which he lived.

Shortly before Jesus rode into Jerusalem on Palm Sunday, he taught his disciples about the end times (Jesus' return to judge the world and to bring down a new heaven and a new earth). In this teaching, Jesus made a comparison between the days of Noah and the day King Jesus returns:

> **"As it was in the days of Noah, so it will be at the coming of the Son of Man. For in the days before the flood, people were eating and drinking, marrying and giving in marriage, up to the day Noah entered the ark; and they knew nothing about what would happen until the flood came and took them all away. That is how it will be at the coming of the Son of Man."** (Matthew 24:37-39)

Jesus pointed out that in the days of Noah, people were going about their daily lives. They were eating and drinking, getting married, having kids, and involved in all the normal activities of life. Then Jesus said something interesting:

"They knew *nothing* about what would happen until the flood came and took them all away." Even if Noah's neighbors thought he was a crazy man for building an ark on dry ground, they were not aware that God was going to send a flood, and they didn't know when it would occur. That was Jesus' point in making the comparison to the day he returns. No one, other than God himself, knows when that day will come.

Another reference to Noah is in the book of Hebrews in chapter 11, the "Great Faith" chapter of the Bible. The writer to the Hebrews wrote: **"By faith Noah, when warned about things not yet seen, in holy fear built an ark to save his family. By his faith he condemned the world and became heir of the righteousness that is in keeping with faith"** (verse 7).

What does "by faith" mean? Well, the author of Hebrews gave a great definition in the first verse of that chapter: **"Now faith is confidence in what we hope for and assurance about what we do not see."** The Lord God warned Noah about something that was in the future—namely, the destruction of the planet through a worldwide flood. In holy fear, Noah got to work and started building the ark. Holy fear stands in reverence and awe to God's Word, his will, and his commands. Holy fear is totally different than unholy or unbelieving fear. Unholy fear intimidates and incapacitates a person. Unholy fear stands in stark contrast to faith. By faith and with holy fear, Noah built the ark. Not fear of the people in his culture. Only holy fear of God.

But Noah also did something else: **"By his faith he condemned the world"** (Hebrews 11:7). Noah judged the people of his culture as being guilty of not believing in or following the true God. He rendered a verdict of guilt and condemnation because of the corruption and violence in his culture. Noah was a minority voice in his culture. He was an exile. And he did this because his holy fear of God surpassed any fear he had of his neighbors.

The apostle Peter, in his second letter, echoed the author of the book of Hebrews:

> **For if God did not spare angels when they sinned, but sent them to hell, putting them in chains of darkness to be held for judgment; if he did not spare the ancient world when he brought the flood on its ungodly people, but protected Noah, a preacher of righteousness, and seven others . . .** (2:4,5)

Peter described Noah as a "preacher of righteousness." The Greek word translated as "preacher" is a derivative of another Greek word that means "to announce publicly religious truth while encouraging people to accept and comply with that truth." There was nothing passive about Noah's preaching. He proclaimed God's truth and God's will openly and publicly.

The fourth and final New Testament reference to Noah is found in 1 Peter 3:19–22:

> **After being made alive, he went and made proclamation to the imprisoned spirits—to those who were disobedient long ago when God waited patiently in the days of Noah while the ark was being built. In it only a few people, eight in all, were saved through water, and this water symbolizes baptism that now saves you also—not the removal of dirt from the body but the pledge of a clear conscience toward God. It saves you by the resurrection of Jesus Christ, who has gone into heaven and is at God's right hand—with angels, authorities and powers in submission to him.**

Here Peter compared how Noah and his family were saved through water with the waters of Baptism, which save us because of Jesus' life, death, and resurrection.

Noah lived as an exile in a culture that was corrupt and violent. He was torn like anyone else between getting along with the culture around him or being obedient to the Lord God. Unlike the vast majority of the people in his culture, he chose the latter. Noah lived counter to the culture. He chose to fear the Lord God, who had the power to create the world and the power to destroy it. It's good to remind ourselves that our God still has that power. He is still in control.

Yet Noah did more than just passively live his life as an exile in a godless culture. He took advantage of the opportunity that the Lord God had given him. He was a preacher of righteousness. He openly and publicly proclaimed God's truth, his Word, and his will. He pointed out the wickedness and evil in his culture. He warned about God's judgment upon the people of his day who chose evil and violence over obedience to the Lord God.

## GOD'S TRUTH FOR MY LIFE

The culture in which we live is comprised of numerous categories that shape it. These categories include government, business, education, religion, media, technology, arts and entertainment, and social norms (what's accepted in society). All these categories contribute to making our culture what it is.

Noah lived in a culture filled with corruption (things ruined) and violence. Compare the culture of Noah's day with ours. In each of the cultural categories listed below, identify one or two aspects of our culture that have been ruined (corrupted) and/or are impacted by violence.

- Government
- Business
- Education
- Religion
- Media
- Science and Technology
- Arts and Entertainment
- Social Norms

Noah was a "preacher of righteousness." He proclaimed publicly God's truth while encouraging people to accept and comply with God's truth.

- To whom do you have the opportunity to proclaim God's truth? List the individuals or groups in your circle of influence.

- What are the ways that you make that proclamation?

- What other opportunities do you have to make a public proclamation of God's truth? Are you willing to seize those opportunities?

We live as exiles in our culture. We live counter to our culture. We live lives torn, just like Noah.

With our culture's corruption and violence in mind . . .

- Describe how your *faith* overrules the *fear* generated by our culture.

- Describe how your *hope* overcomes the *despair* around us.

- Describe how your *love* for God and people overpowers the *hate* that is prevalent in our culture.

CHAPTER 3

# ABRAHAM AND ISAAC

Are you familiar with a chapter in the New Testament that summarizes many of the major historical events of the Old Testament? It is in Acts chapter 7. The chapter contains a speech by a man named Stephen who addressed the Sanhedrin, the Jewish ruling council.

In the previous chapter of Acts, we meet Stephen for the first time. He was one of the seven men chosen to oversee the daily distribution of food to the Grecian widows in Jerusalem. As we read on, we learn more about Stephen's character, gifts, and work:

> **Now Stephen, a man full of God's grace and power, performed great wonders and signs among the people. Opposition arose, however, from members of the Synagogue of the Freedmen (as it was called)—Jews of Cyrene and Alexandria as well as the provinces of Cilicia and Asia—who began to argue with Stephen. But they could not stand up against the wisdom the Spirit gave him as he spoke.**

**Then they secretly persuaded some men to say, "We have heard Stephen speak blasphemous words against Moses and against God."**

**So they stirred up the people and the elders and the teachers of the law. They seized Stephen and brought him before the Sanhedrin. They produced false witnesses, who testified, "This fellow never stops speaking against this holy place and against the law. For we have heard him say that this Jesus of Nazareth will destroy this place and change the customs Moses handed down to us."**

**All who were sitting in the Sanhedrin looked intently at Stephen, and they saw that his face was like the face of an angel.** (Acts 6:8–15)

Stephen was an incredible leader and follower of Jesus. Since he was filled with the Spirit and the Spirit's wisdom, he was courageous and compelling in his confession. The enemies of Stephen had persuaded some men to accuse him falsely of blasphemy. That charge resulted in Stephen being brought before the Sanhedrin.

In his speech to the Sanhedrin, Stephen spoke about Abraham and his life in exile:

**"Brothers and fathers, listen to me! The God of glory appeared to our father Abraham while he was**

**still in Mesopotamia, before he lived in Harran. 'Leave your country and your people,' God said, 'and go to the land I will show you.'**

**"So he left the land of the Chaldeans and settled in Harran. After the death of his father, God sent him to this land where you are now living. He gave him no inheritance here, not even enough ground to set his foot on. But God promised him that he and his descendants after him would possess the land, even though at that time Abraham had no child."** (Acts 7:2–5)

Abraham, by birth, was known as Abram. He lived about two thousand years before Jesus was born. He grew up in a family that did not know the Lord God. The clan of his father, Terah, originated in Ur of the Chaldees. Bible scholars aren't in agreement as to whether Ur was a specific city or a word that meant "land"—namely, "land of the Chaldees." Ur, or the land of the Chaldees, was located in the lower Mesopotamia region. This region was on one end of the Fertile Crescent, a crescent shape (think boomerang shape) that extended from the Persian Gulf to Egypt, wrapping around to the north of the Arabian Desert. Today, the lower Mesopotamia region includes the small country of Kuwait and the southern part of Iraq, just northwest of the Persian Gulf.

Terah decided one day to take Abram; Abram's wife,

Sarai; and his nephew Lot and move to Canaan. The journey took them from the southern part of the Fertile Crescent to the very northern part of the Fertile Crescent. Terah and his clan never made it to Canaan as planned. They stopped in Haran and settled there. Haran was (and still is) a town located in what today is southeastern Turkey. Haran was located on the main east/west road that connected Nineveh in the east to Carchemish in the west.

When Abram was 75 years old, the Lord came to him with a message: **"Go from your country, your people and your father's household to the land I will show you"** (Genesis 12:1). Abram took his wife, Sarai; his nephew Lot; and all their possessions and headed south to Canaan. The land of Canaan was on the eastern shore of the Mediterranean Sea, extending from Lebanon in the north to Egypt in the south and to the Jordan River Valley in the east. Today Lebanon, Israel, and parts of Jordan and Syria occupy the same real estate as the ancient land of Canaan.

When Abram's family arrived in Canaan, the Lord again came to Abram and made him a promise: **"To your offspring I will give this land"** (Genesis 12:7). Someday, Abram's descendants would occupy the land. For the time being and for his entire life, Abram would live as an exile in the land of Canaan, which, not surprisingly, was occupied by the Canaanites.

The Canaanites are mentioned more than 150 times in the Bible. In some cases, the word *Canaanites* refers to a specific group of people who lived either on the east side of the Jordan

River or along the coastal lowlands of the Mediterranean. In other cases, the word *Canaanites* refers to all the inhabitants of the land of Canaan. You see, other tribes lived in the land of Canaan too. They were people known as the Amorites, Hittites, Amalekites, Hivites, Jebusites, Girgashites, and Perrizites, among others.

The Canaanites were descendants of Canaan, Noah's grandson. Canaan and his descendants were a brutal and wicked people who did not worship the Lord God (Yahweh Elohim). They worshiped idols like Baal, Asherah, and Molech. They lived in fortified cities scattered throughout the land. They were also known for their larger physical size and their fighting fierceness. This made the Canaanite peoples intimidating to outsiders. Their culture was permeated with all kinds of sexual immorality (homosexuality, incest, and bestiality) and child sacrifice. Probably the darkest example of sexual immortality during the life of Abram was what was going on in the cities of Sodom and Gomorrah.

The Canaanites stood opposed to everything that the Lord God stood for. That's why, years later, the Lord God would tell Joshua to eliminate all the Canaanites. They were an abomination to him. The Lord God also didn't want them influencing his chosen people. If they remained in the land, the Lord God knew that the Israelites would eventually succumb to their idolatry and all the detestable practices of the Canaanites. Unfortunately, God's people allowed many of the Canaanites to live and remain in the land. Guess what happened? More on this in a bit.

When Abram and his family came to Canaan, they initially settled in the southern part of the land, called the Negev. In the course of time, there was a severe famine in the land of Canaan. So Abram temporarily moved from being an exile in Canaan to being an exile in Egypt. What happened in Egypt sadly revealed Abram's lack of trust in God's providence and revealed some unsettling aspects of the Egyptian culture.

Before entering Egypt, Abram told his wife, Sarai (her name would later be changed to Sarah), to tell people she was his sister, not his wife. Because Sarai was such a beautiful woman, Abram was afraid that someone would kill him in order to steal Sarai as his own wife. In doing so, Abram revealed his lack of trust. But it also revealed the real possibility that an Egyptian man would be willing to commit murder to get a beautiful woman for himself. To us, that seems like a cultural extreme.

Abram didn't get murdered, but Sarai ended up in Pharaoh's harem at the recommendation of Pharaoh's officials. Pharaoh took Sarai to be one of his wives:

> **He** [Pharaoh] **treated Abram well for her sake, and Abram acquired sheep and cattle, male and female donkeys, male and female servants, and camels.**
>
> **But the Lord inflicted serious diseases on Pharaoh and his household because of Abram's wife Sarai. So Pharaoh summoned Abram. "What have you**

> **done to me?" he said. "Why didn't you tell me she was your wife? Why did you say, 'She is my sister,' so that I took her to be my wife? Now then, here is your wife. Take her and go!" Then Pharaoh gave orders about Abram to his men, and they sent him on his way, with his wife and everything he had.** (Genesis 12:16–20)

It appears that Egyptian culture placed a low value on God's gift of life as well as God's gift of sex and marriage. Following this kerfuffle, Pharaoh sent Abram, Sarai, and all Abram's servants away.

Did you know that Abram (after his name was changed to Abraham) had a second "Sister-Sarah" moment? Abraham tried to pass off Sarah as his sister to the city-state king of Gerar, a city in Philistia. The king's name was Abimelek. And did you know that Abraham's son Isaac would one day try to pass off his beautiful wife, Rebekah, as his sister and that he tried to do it with the very same king of Gerar, Abimelek? Seriously. Like father, like son.

Abram and his clan left Egypt and returned to the Negev, the southernmost part of the land of Canaan. At this point, **"Abram had become very wealthy in livestock and in silver and gold"** (Genesis 13:2). In fact, because of the size of his livestock and the livestock of his nephew Lot, it was time for each to find their own grazing land. Abram told Lot, "You pick. If you want to go east, I'll go west, or vice versa." Lot chose the plains along the Jordan River near Sodom. So

Abram moved his tents to Hebron, which was located in south-central Canaan.

The Lord God had told Abram that the land of Canaan would be the home of his descendants. But Abram and Sarai were still childless. So Sarai came up with a plan. She offered her servant, Hagar, to Abram to see if she could give him a child. Hagar became pregnant and gave birth to a son, whose name was Ishmael. Abram was 86 years old when Ishmael was born. It is apparent that in Abram's day, God's original idea of marriage—one man, one woman, for life—wasn't followed, even among followers of the Lord God.

When Abram was 99 years old (and with no offspring yet), the Lord God changed his name from Abram, which means "exalted father," to Abraham, which means "father of many." Within the year, Abraham would have a son. The Lord God also changed Sarai's name, which means "my princess," to Sarah, a name that also means "princess" but in a wider sense. With her name change, she wouldn't just be Abraham's princess but the princess to the *many* promised to father Abraham.

With the name change of Sarai to Sarah, the Lord God also made a promise. The Lord said:

> **"I will bless her and will surely give you a son by her. I will bless her so that she will be the mother of nations; kings of peoples will come from her."**
>
> **Abraham fell facedown; he laughed and said to**

> **himself, "Will a son be born to a man a hundred years old? Will Sarah bear a child at the age of ninety?" And Abraham said to God, "If only Ishmael might live under your blessing!"**
>
> **Then God said, "Yes, but your wife Sarah will bear you a son, and you will call him Isaac. I will establish my covenant with him as an everlasting covenant for his descendants after him."** (Genesis 17:16–19)

Within the year, Sarah would give birth to a son. The new parents gave him the name Isaac, a name that means "he laughs."

Shortly after the Lord God made that promise to Abraham, three visitors came to his tent to repeat that promise. One was the Lord himself, and the other two were angels. All three appeared as human beings who ate and drank the meal that Sarah had prepared. Sarah heard the Lord tell Abraham that within the year she would have a son. And what did Sarah do in response? She laughed.

The three visitors not only came to give a birth announcement; they came to carry out God's judgment on the cities of Sodom and Gomorrah. The Lord continued to talk to Abraham, who pleaded for the righteous people living in the two cities. One reason was because Abraham's nephew Lot and his family likely lived in Sodom. As the two angels were about to leave, the Lord said to Abraham, **"The outcry**

**against Sodom and Gomorrah is so great and their sin so grievous"** (Genesis 18:20).

So what was the sin of Sodom and Gomorrah? Actually, we should say *sins* because there were more than just one. The two angels arrived in the evening. They met Lot who was sitting at the city gate. Although the angels had planned to spend the night in the town square, Lot insisted that they have some dinner at his home and spend the night inside. What happened next reveals one of the grievous sins that would result in the two cities being destroyed.

> **Before they had gone to bed, all the men from every part of the city of Sodom—both young and old—surrounded the house. They called to Lot, "Where are the men who came to you tonight? Bring them out to us so that we can have sex with them."**
>
> **Lot went outside to meet them and shut the door behind him and said, "No, my friends. Don't do this wicked thing. Look, I have two daughters who have never slept with a man. Let me bring them out to you, and you can do what you like with them. But don't do anything to these men, for they have come under the protection of my roof."** (Genesis 19:4–8)

One of the sins of Sodom and Gomorrah was the sin of homosexuality. The name of the city of Sodom has given us the term *sodomy*, which means "sex between two men, either forced or consensual." There is no doubt that homosexuality was one of the reasons why God destroyed these two cities. But it wasn't the only reason.

Another related sin was what Lot suggested—allowing the men of the city to rape his two daughters. Heterosexual sins also abounded in these two cities, in part because women were considered property in that culture and, at best, second-class citizens.

The book of Ezekiel also gives some insight into the sins of Sodom and Gomorrah:

> **"Now this was the sin of your sister Sodom: She and her daughters were arrogant, overfed and unconcerned; they did not help the poor and needy. They were haughty and did detestable things before me. Therefore I did away with them as you have seen."** (16:49,50)

So, the sins of Sodom included pride, complacency, apathy, a lack of concern for the underprivileged in society, and arrogance, in addition to the sins of homosexuality and other heterosexual sins.

When Lot confronted the men outside of his home, it was clear they wanted in to get to the visitors in his home. When they pushed forward on the front door, the angels reached out and pulled Lot back inside. The angels then blinded the mob of men, which allowed Lot, his wife, and his two daughters to leave the city with the angels. When they had gotten a safe distance away, the Lord God rained down fire and brimstone on the cities of Sodom and Gomorrah and destroyed them.

As the three visitors to Abraham's tent had indicated, Isaac was born to Abraham and Sarah within the year. Then we fast-forward 40 years. When Isaac was 40 years old, Abraham arranged for Isaac's marriage:

> **Abraham was now very old, and the Lord had blessed him in every way. He said to the senior servant in his household, the one in charge of all that he had, "Put your hand under my thigh. I want you to swear by the Lord, the God of heaven and the God of earth, that you will not get a wife for my son from the daughters of the Canaanites, among whom I am living, but will go to my country and my own relatives and get a wife for my son Isaac."**
> (Genesis 24:1-4)

Abraham acknowledged with both words and actions that he was living as an exile in the land of Canaan. Abraham sent his senior servant back to Haran to find a wife for Isaac. And Abraham made him swear an oath that he would not find a wife from among the Canaanites. The servant went and found a wife for Isaac. Her name was Rebekah. She was Abraham's great-niece.

In the culture of the day, arranged marriages were common. But what stood out in this marriage arrangement was the insistence by Abraham that Isaac marry a woman from his own clan and not a Canaanite woman.

The Lord God promised the land of Canaan to Abraham's offspring. That meant that for the rest of his life, Abraham would live in exile while living in the Land of Promise. So would his son Isaac and his grandson Jacob. Keep in mind that for these three patriarchs, living in exile wasn't their idea.

It was God's idea.

## GOD'S TRUTH FOR MY LIFE

The culture in which Abraham and Isaac lived did not value God's gift of life and God's gift of sex and marriage in the way God values them. Identify three to five examples each of how our current culture does not value these gifts from God. Then consider what you, as a Christian who values these gifts, can do to change cultural attitudes.

**God's Gift of Life**

-
-
-
-
-

## God's Gifts of Sex and Marriage

- 
- 
- 
- 
- 

Abraham arranged the marriage of Isaac and Rebekah because he didn't want Isaac marrying a Canaanite woman who didn't believe in the Lord God.

- Can you identify any benefits if we had arranged marriages in our culture?
- Since arranged marriages aren't part of our culture, can you identify any steps you can take with your children or grandchildren to achieve the same goal that Abraham had for Isaac?

Abraham and Isaac both had some trust issues with the words and promises of God. They feared for their lives because they thought someone might want to kill them in order to take their beautiful wives.

- With what promises of God do you struggle?

- What steps can you take to overcome your lack of trust in God's promises?

We live as exiles in our culture. We live counter to our culture. We live lives torn, just like Abraham and Isaac.

When it comes to God's gift of life and God's gifts of sex and marriage . . .

- Describe how your *faith* overrules the *fear* generated by our culture.

- Describe how your *hope* overcomes the *despair* around us.

- Describe how your *love* for God and people overpowers the *hate* that is prevalent in our culture.

CHAPTER 4

# JACOB AND JOSEPH

In Stephen's speech to the Sanhedrin, he described another exile that involved God's Old Testament people. Stephen summarized approximately five hundred years of history after Abraham lived with these words:

> **"God spoke to him** [Abraham] **in this way: 'For four hundred years your descendants will be strangers in a country not their own, and they will be enslaved and mistreated. But I will punish the nation they serve as slaves,' God said, 'and afterward they will come out of that country and worship me in this place.'"** (Acts 7:6,7)

Then Stephen recounted the details of these five centuries, with 430 years of God's people living in exile in Egypt. Although this is a longer section of Scripture, it's worth knowing. Stephen gave us an overview of Jacob and his 12 sons living in exile while living in the world:

**"Then he gave Abraham the covenant of circumcision. And Abraham became the father of Isaac and circumcised him eight days after his birth. Later Isaac became the father of Jacob, and Jacob became the father of the twelve patriarchs.**

**"Because the patriarchs were jealous of Joseph, they sold him as a slave into Egypt. But God was with him and rescued him from all his troubles. He gave Joseph wisdom and enabled him to gain the goodwill of Pharaoh king of Egypt. So Pharaoh made him ruler over Egypt and all his palace.**

**"Then a famine struck all Egypt and Canaan, bringing great suffering, and our ancestors could not find food. When Jacob heard that there was grain in Egypt, he sent our forefathers on their first visit. On their second visit, Joseph told his brothers who he was, and Pharaoh learned about Joseph's family. After this, Joseph sent for his father Jacob and his whole family, seventy-five in all. Then Jacob went down to Egypt, where he and our ancestors died. Their bodies were brought back to Shechem and placed in the tomb that Abraham had bought from the sons of Hamor at Shechem for a certain sum of money."** (Acts 7:8-16)

Other than Isaac's "Sister-Rebekah" moment with

Abimelek, the Bible doesn't record much about the culture during Isaac's life. Most of what we read in Genesis is about Isaac's family and their internal challenges and opportunities. And there were many.

For example, there was the caustic relationship between Esau and Jacob, the twin sons of Isaac and Rebekah. There was the conniving relationship between Jacob and his Uncle Laban. There were the imbalanced love relationships between Jacob; his two wives, Leah and Rachel; and his wives' servants, Zilpah and Bilhah. There was the feuding relationship between the sisters, Rachel and Leah. There was the broken relationship between Laban and his daughters as they returned with Jacob to Laban's home. Finally, there were the restored relationships between Jacob and Esau and between Jacob and Isaac. These were all important events in the patriarchs' lives, but they were all internal, family-centered events.

We don't gain greater insight into living as exiles in the Canaanite culture (and eventually the Egyptian culture) until we get to the next generation—Jacob's 12 sons.

Genesis chapter 37 begins with a short summary of Jacob's life and introduces us to one of his sons:

**Jacob lived in the land where his father had stayed, the land of Canaan.**

**This is the account of Jacob's family line.**

> **Joseph, a young man of seventeen, was tending the flocks with his brothers, the sons of Bilhah and the sons of Zilpah, his father's wives, and he brought their father a bad report about them.**
>
> **Now Israel loved Joseph more than any of his other sons, because he had been born to him in his old age; and he made an ornate robe for him. When his brothers saw that their father loved him more than any of them, they hated him and could not speak a kind word to him.** (verses 1–4)

Jacob (or Israel) fostered hatred between the brothers and Joseph by giving Joseph an ornate robe that screamed "special," "favorite son," "loved more than anyone." Joseph also fostered his brothers' hatred in his own way:

> **Joseph had a dream, and when he told it to his brothers, they hated him all the more. He said to them, "Listen to this dream I had: We were binding sheaves of grain out in the field when suddenly my sheaf rose and stood upright, while your sheaves gathered around mine and bowed down to it."**
>
> **His brothers said to him, "Do you intend to reign over us? Will you actually rule us?" And they hated him all the more because of his dream and what he had said.**

**Then he had another dream, and he told it to his brothers. "Listen," he said, "I had another dream, and this time the sun and moon and eleven stars were bowing down to me."** (Genesis 37:5-9)

The first dream pictured the brothers bowing down to Joseph. The second dream pictured the same except that Joseph's father and mother would bow down as well. Jacob questioned Joseph about this dream, but he also tucked the conversation away in the back of his memory. Because of the dreams, the brothers hated Joseph all the more. It became so intense that they decided to kill their younger brother.

One day Jacob told Joseph to go and see how his brothers were doing tending the flocks. So Joseph went after his brothers and found them near Dothan. But they saw him in the distance, and before he reached them, they plotted to kill him.

**"Here comes that dreamer!" they said to each other. "Come now, let's kill him and throw him into one of these cisterns and say that a ferocious animal devoured him. Then we'll see what comes of his dreams."** (Genesis 37:19,20)

When Reuben (the oldest brother) heard about the plan, he suggested not killing Joseph but just leaving him in the cistern. Reuben had the idea of circling back and rescuing Joseph from the cistern and taking him back to his father.

When Joseph arrived, the brothers stripped him of his robe and threw him into the cistern.

Then they sat down to have lunch. Imagine that! Throwing your brother into a cistern to die and then sitting down to have lunch! As they were eating, a caravan came by. Judah suggested a change of plans. The brothers decided not to kill their brother but rather sold him to some Ishmaelites and Midianites, who took Joseph with them to Egypt.

It seems that the brothers considered murder a more serious act than human trafficking, so they opted to sell their brother into slavery rather than to kill him.

Who were the Ishmaelites and Midianites? Both are mentioned in this account. Are they one and the same? Some Bible scholars think so. Or are they different groups of people? Other Bible scholars differentiate between the two. Let's first look at their origins. Ishmaelites were descendants of Ishmael, who was the son of Abraham and Hagar, Sarah's servant. Midianites were descendants of Midian, a son of Abraham and his second wife, Keturah. Abraham had married Keturah after Sarah died. So the Ishmaelites and the Midianites were both descended from Abraham, but they were different groups of people because they had a different ancestral mother. So why are both mentioned?

The best explanation comes as the result of how both groups are described. **"They** [the brothers] **looked up and saw a caravan of Ishmaelites coming from Gilead. Their camels were loaded"** (Genesis 37:25). You see, the camels were owned by the Ishmaelites. Then in the verse 28 it says, **"So**

**when the Midianite merchants came by . . ."** The Midianites are described as the merchants, the ones who were selling the spices, balm, and myrrh. So it seems that the Ishmaelites were the freight company, and the Midianites were the merchants.

No matter what, the Ishmaelites and Midianites were involved in commerce, one category that influences the culture in which we live. For the most part, commerce is an aspect of our culture that is typically neutral. But in this case, commerce included human trafficking and slavery.

With the selling of Joseph into slavery, Joseph's brothers then inflicted one additional act of cruelty, this time upon their father:

> **Then they got Joseph's robe, slaughtered a goat and dipped the robe in the blood. They took the ornate robe back to their father and said, "We found this. Examine it to see whether it is your son's robe."**
>
> **He recognized it and said, "It is my son's robe! Some ferocious animal has devoured him. Joseph has surely been torn to pieces."**
>
> **Then Jacob tore his clothes, put on sackcloth and mourned for his son many days. All his sons and daughters came to comfort him, but he refused to be comforted. "No," he said, "I will continue to mourn until I join my son in the grave." So his father wept for him.**

**Meanwhile, the Midianites sold Joseph in Egypt to Potiphar, one of Pharaoh's officials, the captain of the guard.** (Genesis 37:31-36)

The deception on their father was the rotten fruit of their hatred for Joseph. That hatred had been ignited by a flame of favoritism on the part of their father and multiplied by the arrogant, jealousy-producing actions of Joseph. As a result, Joseph went from being in exile in the land of Canaan to being an exile *and* a slave in the land of Egypt.

The following years were an up and down roller-coaster ride for Joseph. Joseph experienced numerous challenges but also significant opportunities. He was sold as a slave to Potiphar, the captain of the guard for the pharaoh of Egypt. The Lord God blessed Joseph by giving him success in everything he did. Potiphar recognized this and put Joseph in charge of his entire estate. This was a blessing for Joseph, especially because he was a foreigner and a slave. Roller coaster *up*.

But then Potiphar's wife tried to seduce Joseph. When Joseph refused her advances, she implicated Joseph in a lie to her husband: **"That Hebrew slave you brought us came to me to make sport of me. But as soon as I screamed for help, he left his cloak beside me and ran out of the house"** (Genesis 39:17,18). Not surprisingly, Potiphar was angry and had Joseph put in the prison where Pharaoh held his prisoners. Roller coaster *down*.

**But while Joseph was there in the prison, the Lord**

**was with him; he showed him kindness and granted him favor in the eyes of the prison warden. So the warden put Joseph in charge of all those held in the prison, and he was made responsible for all that was done there. The warden paid no attention to anything under Joseph's care, because the LORD was with Joseph and gave him success in whatever he did.** (Genesis 39:20–23)

Roller coaster *up*.

One day two of Pharaoh's officials, the chief cupbearer and the chief baker, showed up at the prison and were put under Joseph's charge by the captain of the guard. For some reason, Pharaoh was angry with both of them. Sometime later, both officials each had a dream on the same night that troubled both of them to the point that they were visibly distraught. Joseph asked them why they were dejected. They indicated that they both had dreams but didn't know what the dreams meant.

Joseph, after reminding the cupbearer and the baker that God is the one who interprets dreams, explained what each dream meant. The dream of the chief cupbearer meant that in three days Pharaoh would restore him to his position. Joseph then asked a favor: **"But when all goes well with you, remember me and show me kindness; mention me to Pharaoh and get me out of this prison. I was forcibly carried off from the land of the Hebrews, and even here I have done nothing to deserve being put in a dungeon"**

(Genesis 40:14,15). The meaning of the dream of the chief baker wasn't as good. His dream meant that in three days he would be put to death by order of the king.

In three days, both events happened. The chief cupbearer was restored to his position, and the chief baker was hanged. But the chief cupbearer immediately forgot about Joseph. Roller coaster *down*.

Joseph spent another two years in the dungeon until the day when Pharaoh had two dreams that none of his magicians and wise men could interpret. It was at that point that the chief cupbearer remembered Joseph and informed Pharaoh about Joseph's ability to interpret dreams. Pharaoh summoned Joseph immediately, after Joseph first had a shave, likely a bath, and as the Bible indicates, a change of clothes.

When Joseph came before the Egyptian king, **"Pharaoh said to Joseph, 'I had a dream, and no one can interpret it. But I have heard it said of you that when you hear a dream you can interpret it.' 'I cannot do it,' Joseph replied to Pharaoh, 'but God will give Pharaoh the answer he desires'"** (Genesis 41:15,16).

Pharaoh shared his two dreams with Joseph:

> **Pharaoh said to Joseph, "In my dream I was standing on the bank of the Nile, when out of the river there came up seven cows, fat and sleek, and they grazed among the reeds. After them, seven other cows came up—scrawny and very ugly and lean. I had never seen such ugly cows in all the land of**

**Egypt. The lean, ugly cows ate up the seven fat cows that came up first. But even after they ate them, no one could tell that they had done so; they looked just as ugly as before. Then I woke up.**

**"In my dream I saw seven heads of grain, full and good, growing on a single stalk. After them, seven other heads sprouted—withered and thin and scorched by the east wind. The thin heads of grain swallowed up the seven good heads. I told this to the magicians, but none of them could explain it to me."**

**Then Joseph said to Pharaoh, "The dreams of Pharaoh are one and the same. God has revealed to Pharaoh what he is about to do. The seven good cows are seven years, and the seven good heads of grain are seven years; it is one and the same dream. The seven lean, ugly cows that came up afterward are seven years, and so are the seven worthless heads of grain scorched by the east wind: They are seven years of famine."** (Genesis 41:17–27)

After interpreting Pharaoh's two dreams, Joseph recommended a plan for managing the seven years of abundance so there would be grain during the seven years of famine.

**Then Pharaoh said to Joseph, "Since God has made all this known to you, there is no one so discerning**

> **and wise as you. You shall be in charge of my palace, and all my people are to submit to your orders. Only with respect to the throne will I be greater than you."** (Genesis 41:39,40)

Roller coaster *up. Way up.*

With Joseph's new position, we get a small glimpse into Egyptian culture:

> **Then Pharaoh took his signet ring from his finger and put it on Joseph's finger. He dressed him in robes of fine linen and put a gold chain around his neck. He had him ride in a chariot as his second-in-command, and people shouted before him, "Make way!" Thus he put him in charge of the whole land of Egypt.**
>
> **Then Pharaoh said to Joseph, "I am Pharaoh, but without your word no one will lift hand or foot in all Egypt." Pharaoh gave Joseph the name Zaphenath-Paneah and gave him Asenath daughter of Potiphera, priest of On, to be his wife. And Joseph went throughout the land of Egypt.**
>
> **Joseph was thirty years old when he entered the service of Pharaoh king of Egypt. And Joseph went out from Pharaoh's presence and traveled throughout Egypt.** (Genesis 41:42-46)

Joseph was a 30-year old exile in Egypt. He was exiled from his father and the rest of his family. Yet as an exile, he became the number-two ruler in all of Egypt. Pharaoh showered him with the outward trappings of being the second-in-command—jewelry, robes of fine linen, and his own personal chariot. He was given authority and power over the entire nation. Pharaoh also gave him a new name, an Egyptian name. Joseph faithfully served Pharaoh in the role he had been given. Yet he remained faithful to the Lord God. Joseph lived in two worlds. He lived *in* Pharaoh's world, but he was not *of* that world. He was an exile and, as a result, lived life torn.

Joseph successfully managed the seven years of abundance in order to have grain for the seven years of famine, not only for the land of Egypt but also for the other nations affected by the famine:

> **During the seven years of abundance the land produced plentifully. Joseph collected all the food produced in those seven years of abundance in Egypt and stored it in the cities. In each city he put the food grown in the fields surrounding it. Joseph stored up huge quantities of grain, like the sand of the sea; it was so much that he stopped keeping records because it was beyond measure.** (Genesis 41:47-49)

When the famine arrived, Joseph opened up the

storehouses and sold grain to both Egyptians and people from other countries. The biblical text points out that **"the famine was severe everywhere. When Jacob learned that there was grain in Egypt, he said to his sons, '. . . Go down there and buy some for us'"** (Genesis 41:57–42:2).

So ten of Joseph's brothers traveled to Egypt. The youngest brother, Benjamin, did not go with them. Jacob was afraid that harm might come to him. When the brothers arrived in Egypt, they went to the governor who was overseeing the selling of the grain, their brother Joseph. They met Joseph and bowed down to him, fulfilling the dream Joseph had about his brothers. Joseph recognized his brothers, but the brothers didn't recognize Joseph.

Joseph pretended to be a stranger to them and began to speak harshly to them. Joseph accused them of being spies. The brothers defended themselves, saying that they only came to Egypt to buy grain. In the process of their defense, they acknowledged that they were all sons of one man, that there was one more brother at home and **"one is no more"** (Genesis 42:13).

Joseph maintained that they were all spies and that all but one of them would remain in Egypt. The one would return to get the youngest brother and bring him also to Egypt. For three days, Joseph held them in custody. On the third day, Joseph softened his position. He told them that all but one of them could return home but that one of the brothers would remain in Egypt until they brought back with them their youngest brother.

The brothers came to the conclusion that they were being punished for what they had done to Joseph. Because they acknowledged that what they had done was wrong, Joseph temporarily left their presence because their confession brought Joseph to tears.

Joseph had his brother Simeon bound and taken from them. Simeon would be the one to remain in Egypt. Joseph then gave the orders to have their grain sacks filled with grain and the silver, which was used to pay for the grain, secretly put back into the brothers' grain sacks. The brothers returned and told Jacob all that had happened. Jacob was filled with grief because he feared losing Benjamin along with Joseph and Simeon.

When the grain ran out, Jacob told his sons to go to Egypt and buy more. Very reluctantly, with assurances of Benjamin's safety from both Reuben and Judah, Jacob allowed Benjamin to go with them. In addition, Jacob directed the brothers to take along double the amount of silver as well as some gifts—balm, honey, spices, myrrh, pistachio nuts, and almonds. Jacob prayed that God Almighty might allow all of his sons to return.

When the brothers arrived in Egypt and Joseph saw Benjamin with them, he told one of his stewards to bring them to his house and prepare a noontime meal for them. When the brothers acknowledged to the steward that they had found silver in their sacks on their previous trip, the steward replied:

> **"It's all right," he said. "Don't be afraid. Your God, the God of your father, has given you treasure in your sacks; I received your silver." Then he brought Simeon out to them.** (Genesis 43:23)

When Joseph arrived at his home, the brothers presented him with the gifts they had brought and bowed down to the ground before him. Joseph then inquired about their family, especially their youngest brother, Benjamin, with whom Joseph shared a birth mother, Rachel. Joseph was so moved that he left to find a private room, where he wept.

The next verses in chapter 43 reveal some interesting details:

> **They served him by himself, the brothers by themselves, and the Egyptians who ate with him by themselves, because Egyptians could not eat with Hebrews, for that is detestable to Egyptians. The men had been seated before him in the order of their ages, from the firstborn to the youngest; and they looked at each other in astonishment. When portions were served to them from Joseph's table, Benjamin's portion was five times as much as anyone else's. So they feasted and drank freely with him.** (verses 32-34)

Joseph seated his brothers according to age, and they were astonished how that happened. When the food was served, Benjamin received five times as much as anyone else. It seems that Joseph was testing to see if the older brothers displayed any jealousy.

Before the brothers were to return home, Joseph gave instructions to the steward of the house to give his brothers as much grain as they could haul and to put the silver back into each man's sack. In addition, Joseph told the steward to put his own silver cup into the sack of the youngest brother, Benjamin. The next morning the brothers headed for home.

Joseph then told his servants to go after the brothers and bring them back because Benjamin "stole" Joseph's cup. When the silver cup was found in Benjamin's sack, they all returned to the city. When the brothers stood before Joseph, he stated that only the one who had the cup in his bag would become his slave. The rest could return home.

What followed was a sincere, emotional pleading by the brothers to allow Benjamin to return, otherwise their father would die in misery.

Joseph couldn't take it anymore and finally revealed himself to his brothers:

> **"I am Joseph! Is my father still living?" But his brothers were not able to answer him, because they were terrified at his presence.**
>
> **Then Joseph said to his brothers, "Come close to me." When they had done so, he said, "I am your brother Joseph, the one you sold into Egypt! And**

> **now, do not be distressed and do not be angry with yourselves for selling me here, because it was to save lives that God sent me ahead of you. For two years now there has been famine in the land, and for the next five years there will be no plowing and reaping. But God sent me ahead of you to preserve for you a remnant on earth and to save your lives by a great deliverance."** (Genesis 45:3-7)

After an emotional reunion, Joseph directed his brothers to return home and bring their father down to Egypt:

> **When the news reached Pharaoh's palace that Joseph's brothers had come, Pharaoh and all his officials were pleased. Pharaoh said to Joseph, "Tell your brothers, 'Do this: Load your animals and return to the land of Canaan, and bring your father and your families back to me. I will give you the best of the land of Egypt and you can enjoy the fat of the land.'**
>
> **"You are also directed to tell them, 'Do this: Take some carts from Egypt for your children and your wives, and get your father and come. Never mind about your belongings, because the best of all Egypt will be yours.'"** (Genesis 45:16-20)

When Jacob and his clan set out for Egypt, they stopped

at Beersheba, where Jacob offered sacrifices to the God of his father, Isaac. That night Jacob experienced his seventh encounter with the Lord God during his lifetime:

> **God spoke to Israel in a vision at night and said, "Jacob! Jacob!"**
>
> **"Here I am," he replied.**
>
> **"I am God, the God of your father," he said. "Do not be afraid to go down to Egypt, for I will make you into a great nation there. I will go down to Egypt with you, and I will surely bring you back again. And Joseph's own hand will close your eyes."** (Genesis 46:2–4)

God repeated his promise that Jacob's descendants would become a great nation. God would build that nation in the land of Egypt, in a region known as Goshen. God also assured Jacob that his descendants would one day return to the Land of Promise. By the time they would leave Egypt under the leadership of Moses, they would become a great nation of 600,000 men, not counting women and children. But that wouldn't occur for another 430 years.

> **Then Jacob left Beersheba, and Israel's sons took their father Jacob and their children and their wives in the carts that Pharaoh had sent to**

> **transport him. So Jacob and all his offspring went to Egypt, taking with them their livestock and the possessions they had acquired in Canaan. Jacob brought with him to Egypt his sons and grandsons and his daughters and granddaughters—all his offspring.** (Genesis 46:5-7)

Jacob would live with his family in Egypt for 17 more years. Before he died, he requested that he would be buried in the tomb of his fathers at Machpelah in Hebron, in the Land of Promise. When Jacob died, his sons did as their father requested.

As with his father, Isaac, and his grandfather Abraham, Jacob lived as an exile in the land of Canaan. Then through the gracious guiding hand of the Lord God, Jacob and his entire clan moved to Egypt and ended up living in the most fertile part of the nation for raising livestock, the land of Goshen. So how did this happen? It was because of another aspect of ancient Egyptian culture.

After Jacob and his clan arrived and after the emotional reunion of Jacob with his son Joseph:

> **Joseph said to his brothers and to his father's household, "I will go up and speak to Pharaoh and will say to him, 'My brothers and my father's household, who were living in the land of Canaan, have come to me. The men are shepherds; they tend livestock, and they have brought along**

> **their flocks and herds and everything they own.' When Pharaoh calls you in and asks, 'What is your occupation?' you should answer, 'Your servants have tended livestock from our boyhood on, just as our fathers did.' Then you will be allowed to settle in the region of Goshen, for all shepherds are detestable to the Egyptians."** (Genesis 46:31–34)

So Jacob and his descendants would live in the land of Goshen for the next four centuries. They would become a great nation, and the Lord God would raise up a man who would lead that nation out of exile to the land of Canaan, the Land of Promise, promised to Abraham, Isaac, and Jacob.

## GOD'S TRUTH FOR MY LIFE

In the ancient Middle Eastern culture in which the patriarchs lived, human trafficking and slavery were cultural norms. We might not have personal experiences with either one, but they remain a huge problem around the globe.

First, some statistics . . .

**Human Trafficking**

The 2024 *Trafficking in Persons Report* provides detailed statistics on trafficking in persons, highlighting regional differences in victim identification, convictions, and legislative changes:

- **Global:** 133,943 victims identified and 7,115 convictions. There were 14 new or amended pieces of legislation related to trafficking.
- **Africa:** 21,877 victims identified and 758 convictions, with 2 new legislative pieces.
- **East Asia & Pacific:** 6,543 victims identified and 1,802 convictions, with 2 new legislative pieces.
- **Europe:** 32,996 victims identified and 1,667 convictions, with 4 new legislative pieces.
- **Near East:** 3,450 victims identified and 770 convictions, with 2 new legislative pieces.
- **South & Central Asia:** 50,815 victims identified and 1,245 convictions, with no new legislative pieces.
- **Western Hemisphere:** 18,292 victims identified and 873 convictions, with 4 new legislative pieces.[3]

**Slavery**

According to Walk Free, which is an international human rights group focused on the eradication of modern slavery in all its forms in our lifetime, "an estimated 50 million people were living in situations of modern slavery on any given day in 2021, according to the latest Global Estimates of Modern Slavery. Of these people, approximately 27.6 million were in forced labour and 22 million were in forced marriages."[4]

Both human trafficking and slavery still exist in our world, including in North America.

Identify three to five actions that you, as a Christian, can take to fight against both of these atrocious crimes:

- 
- 
- 
- 
- 

The story of Joseph and his brothers teaches us about the power of jealousy and hatred on the one hand and the power of repentance, forgiveness, and grace on the other hand.

- Identify and share an example from your own life of jealousy and/or hatred. How was it resolved?
- If that jealousy and/or hatred has not yet been resolved, what steps do you plan to take so that you can enjoy repentance, forgiveness, and God's grace?

Ancient Egyptian culture separated itself from other

cultures, such as the Hebrew culture where shepherding occurred. Separation from other cultures can have both positive and negative aspects.

- When is it a positive to separate from another culture? Give an example or two.

- When is it a negative to separate from another culture? Give an example or two.

We live as exiles in our culture. We live counter to our culture. We live lives torn, just like Abraham, Isaac, Jacob, and Jacob's sons.

When it comes to dealing with the appalling nature of human trafficking and slavery . . .

- Describe how your *faith* overrules the *fear* generated by our culture.

- Describe how your *hope* overcomes the *despair* around us.

- Describe how your *love* for God and people overpowers the *hate* that is prevalent in our culture.

# CHAPTER 5
# MOSES

A lot can change over the course of four centuries. That was certainly true for the Israelites living in the land of Goshen in northern Egypt. The opening chapter of the book of Exodus tells us about the two biggest changes:

> **Now Joseph and all his brothers and all that generation died, but the Israelites were exceedingly fruitful; they multiplied greatly, increased in numbers and became so numerous that the land was filled with them.**
>
> **Then a new king, to whom Joseph meant nothing, came to power in Egypt. "Look," he said to his people, "the Israelites have become far too numerous for us. Come, we must deal shrewdly with them or they will become even more numerous and, if war breaks out, will join our enemies, fight against us and leave the country."** (1:6–10)

When Jacob and his household migrated to Egypt at Pharaoh's invitation, there were 70 people in the clan. The first big change that occurred was the growth in their numbers. As mentioned in the previous chapter, the Israelites numbered about 600,000 men, not counting the women and children, at the end of their time in Egypt.

The other big change was that there was a new king, a new pharaoh, to whom Joseph meant nothing. Although we can't be sure, it is reasonable to assume that this king was part of a new dynasty. But who was this king? Again, we can't be *absolutely* certain, but between the Bible and archaeological discoveries, we can be *reasonably* certain.

In 1 Kings 6:1 we read, **"In the four hundred and eightieth year after the Israelites came out of Egypt, in the fourth year of Solomon's reign over Israel, in the month of Ziv, the second month, he began to build the temple of the LORD."** Through various archaeological discoveries, most historians agree that the fourth year of Solomon's reign was in or around 966 B.C. Then, if we add 480 years to it, we arrive at 1446 B.C as the year of the Israelites' exodus from Egypt.

In the 16th century B.C, the ruling dynasty in Egypt was the Hyksos, a Semitic tribe. The Egyptian dynasty that drove out the Hyksos was known as the New Kingdom. This dynasty ruled from approximately 1580 to 1085 B.C. So according to this information, the pharaoh who oppressed the Israelites (and who had no idea who Joseph was) would have been Thutmose III. He ruled from approximately 1500 to 1450 B.C. The pharaoh who ruled at the time of the exodus would have been Amenhotep II. He ruled from approximately 1450 to 1425 B.C.

This new king recognized the threats that the Israelites posed to Egypt. The first threat was the continued growth of the Israelite population. The second threat was that if war broke out against Egypt, the Israelites might join the opposition. The Israelites were a double threat to Egypt as a nation and as a culture.

So what was Pharaoh's plan? Well, it was a two-part plan. Part one of the plan was to oppress the Israelites with forced labor, slave labor. The Egyptians were ruthless in how they treated the Israelites. Part two of the plan involved having the Hebrew midwives kill every baby boy at birth by having those baby boys thrown into the Nile River. Pharaoh ordered the genocide of all Israelite baby boys. However, since the Hebrew midwives feared the Lord God more than they feared the king, they didn't kill the baby boys. So the Israelites became even more numerous.

One of those baby boys was born to a husband and wife who were descendants of Jacob's son Levi.

> **When she** [his mother] **saw that he was a fine child, she hid him for three months. But when she could hide him no longer, she got a papyrus basket for him and coated it with tar and pitch. Then she placed the child in it and put it among the reeds along the bank of the Nile.** (Exodus 2:2,3)

We don't know exactly all that is meant by a "fine child," but it includes traits such as being desirable, good, or pleasant.

We learn about the Lord God's rescue plan for this baby boy, who would one day lead the Israelites out of Egypt to the Promised Land:

> **Then Pharaoh's daughter went down to the Nile to bathe, and her attendants were walking along the riverbank. She saw the basket among the reeds and sent her female slave to get it. She opened it and saw the baby. He was crying, and she felt sorry for him. "This is one of the Hebrew babies," she said.**
>
> **Then his sister asked Pharaoh's daughter, "Shall I go and get one of the Hebrew women to nurse the baby for you?"**
>
> **"Yes, go," she answered. So the girl went and got the baby's mother. Pharaoh's daughter said to her, "Take this baby and nurse him for me, and I will pay you." So the woman took the baby and nursed him. When the child grew older, she took him to Pharaoh's daughter and he became her son. She named him Moses, saying, "I drew him out of the water."** (Exodus 2:5–10)

Stephen, whom I've mentioned earlier, in his speech

before the Sanhedrin, provided a few more details about Moses' early life:

> **"At that time Moses was born, and he was no ordinary child. For three months he was cared for by his family. When he was placed outside, Pharaoh's daughter took him and brought him up as her own son. Moses was educated in all the wisdom of the Egyptians and was powerful in speech and action."**
> (Acts 7:20–22)

When Stephen described young Moses as "no ordinary child," it emphasized that he was no ordinary child in the eyes of God.

So Moses, for the first 40 years of his life, lived in Egyptian culture—language, education, social norms, and palace living. Moses was trained to be a leader, powerful in speech and action. Taking action, however, is what resulted in Moses having to flee Egypt to live in a new culture.

There is another New Testament book where we gain additional insights into Moses' earlier life. The book of Hebrews tells us:

> **By faith Moses, when he had grown up, refused to be known as the son of Pharaoh's daughter. He chose to be mistreated along with the people of God rather than to enjoy the fleeting pleasures of sin. He regarded disgrace for the sake of Christ as of**

**greater value than the treasures of Egypt, because he was looking ahead to his reward.** (11:24–26)

Although Moses lived in an Egyptian culture for 40 years, he learned who he really was, a descendant of Abraham, Isaac, and Jacob. He was a member of God's chosen people. He refused to be known as Pharaoh's grandson. He valued his relationship with the Lord more than what palace living offered. He was living *in* Egypt but not *of* Egypt, as an exile.

Back to Stephen's speech. He continued:

**"When Moses was forty years old, he decided to visit his own people, the Israelites. He saw one of them being mistreated by an Egyptian, so he went to his defense and avenged him by killing the Egyptian. Moses thought that his own people would realize that God was using him to rescue them, but they did not. The next day Moses came upon two Israelites who were fighting. He tried to reconcile them by saying, 'Men, you are brothers; why do you want to hurt each other?'**

**"But the man who was mistreating the other pushed Moses aside and said, 'Who made you ruler and judge over us? Are you thinking of killing me as you killed the Egyptian yesterday?' When Moses heard this, he fled to Midian, where he settled as a foreigner and had two sons."** (Acts 7:23–29)

We learn from Stephen about Moses' thought process for killing the Egyptian. Moses thought that his own people would realize that God was using him to rescue them, but they did not. Stephen doesn't tell us how Moses came to understand that God was going to use him—Moses—to rescue God's chosen people, just that he knew it. However, Moses' timetable for rescuing God's people and the Lord God's timetable were separated by 40 years. Moses wouldn't return from Midian to be Israel's rescuer until he was 80 years old.

When Moses arrived in Midian, he sat down by a well. We're told that a priest in Midian had seven daughters who came to the well to draw water for their father's flocks. Along came some shepherds who drove the daughters away. Moses stepped into the situation and rescued the daughters and watered their flocks. As it turned out, Moses was invited to Jethro's home, agreed to stay with him, married his daughter Zipporah, and had a son whom he named **"Gershom, saying, 'I have become a foreigner in a foreign land'"** (Exodus 2:22).

Forty years after Moses fled Egypt to Midian, the Lord showed up one day in a burning bush that didn't burn up. The Lord called Moses to return to Egypt to lead his people out of Egypt. Moses was quite reluctant to go but eventually did. It was now the Lord's timetable and plan to have Moses rescue God's people from the land of Egypt and the oppression of Pharaoh. Moses got on board with God's plan.

We continue with Stephen's account of Moses' life:

**"After forty years had passed, an angel appeared to Moses in the flames of a burning bush in the desert near Mount Sinai. When he saw this, he was amazed at the sight. As he went over to get a closer look, he heard the Lord say: 'I am the God of your fathers, the God of Abraham, Isaac and Jacob.' Moses trembled with fear and did not dare to look.**

**"Then the Lord said to him, 'Take off your sandals, for the place where you are standing is holy ground. I have indeed seen the oppression of my people in Egypt. I have heard their groaning and have come down to set them free. Now come, I will send you back to Egypt.'**

**"This is the same Moses they had rejected with the words, 'Who made you ruler and judge?' He was sent to be their ruler and deliverer by God himself, through the angel who appeared to him in the bush. He led them out of Egypt and performed wonders and signs in Egypt, at the Red Sea and for forty years in the wilderness."** (Acts 7:30-36)

Before Pharaoh would let God's people leave Egypt, he had to be convinced to do so. The way the Lord God convinced Pharaoh to let his people go was through a series of ten plagues. Even before we get to the first plague, we learn about a feature of Egyptian culture. It was the culture's reliance on wise men, sorcerers, and magicians who practiced their secret arts.

Before Moses and Aaron met with Pharaoh:

> **The Lord said to Moses and Aaron, "When Pharaoh says to you, 'Perform a miracle,' then say to Aaron, 'Take your staff and throw it down before Pharaoh,' and it will become a snake."**
>
> **So Moses and Aaron went to Pharaoh and did just as the Lord commanded. Aaron threw his staff down in front of Pharaoh and his officials, and it became a snake. Pharaoh then summoned wise men and sorcerers, and the Egyptian magicians also did the same things by their secret arts: Each one threw down his staff and it became a snake. But Aaron's staff swallowed up their staffs. Yet Pharaoh's heart became hard and he would not listen to them, just as the Lord had said.** (Exodus 7:8-13)

The Egyptian sorcerers and magicians were able to replicate the Lord God's miracle of the staff turned snake by their own secret arts. They were also able to replicate the first two plagues. The first plague was Moses turning the water in Egypt into blood. The Egyptian magicians replicated it. The second plague was frogs everywhere. The Egyptian magicians were able to replicate it too. But when it came to the third plague, the plague of gnats, the Egyptian magicians were not able to replicate it, nor any of the subsequent plagues.

When the Egyptian magicians weren't able to replicate the gnats, they told Pharaoh, **"This is the finger of God"** (Exodus 8:19). Their statement was a stark contrast between God's power and their own. Nevertheless, our cultural take-away is their reliance on sorcerers and magicians practicing their dark, secret arts.

After ten plagues, Pharaoh was ready to let God's people go. After he did, however, he had a change of heart. There went his slave labor. So Pharaoh's army pursued the Israelites, and after the Lord God parted the Red Sea for the Israelites to travel through safely, he unparted the Red Sea. The walls of water came crashing down on the pursuing Egyptian army, killing them all. Moses and the Israelites would never again live as exiles in Egypt.

From Egypt, Moses led the Israelites to Mt. Sinai, where they received God's Covenant and then to the southern doorstep of the land of Canaan. Moses sent 12 spies into the land that the Lord God had unequivocally promised to the patriarchs. This land was theirs! No ifs, ands, or buts. However, the spies returned with a mixed report. Only two of the spies, Joshua and Caleb, returned with a "God's got this!" report. The other ten spies gave a "Woe is us!" report. As a result of the people's lack of trust in the Lord God's power to defeat every city in the land, the Lord God would let them wander in the wilderness for the next 40 years. Every

Israelite adult, except for Joshua and Caleb, would die in the desert before reaching the Promised Land.

Abraham and his son Isaac lived in exile in the land of Canaan, the Land of Promise. Jacob also lived in exile in the land of Canaan and then as an exile in the land of Egypt. Moses lived in exile in the land of Egypt for 40 years. Then after killing an Egyptian, he fled to Midian and lived as an exile in the land of Midian for another 40 years. Then one day the Lord God spoke to him from out of a burning bush to lead his people out of Egypt to the Land of Promise.

For Abraham, Isaac, Jacob, Jacob's sons, and Moses, living in exile wasn't their idea. It was God's idea. It was all part of his plan to bless his people.

## GOD'S TRUTH FOR MY LIFE

Pharaoh tried to commit genocide against the Hebrew people. The definition of *genocide* is "the deliberate and systematic destruction of a racial, political, or cultural group."[5]

List two or three examples of genocides that have occurred in history. Can you identify any attempted genocides that are occurring in our world today, whether racial, political, or against a particular culture group? What can Christ followers do to combat genocide?

Moses knew that the Lord God would one day have him lead the Israelites out of Egypt. But Moses' timetable didn't align with God's timetable. Moses was 40 years too early. Can you share an example from your own life or the life of someone you know who had to wait on God's timetable for something important to happen?

In Egyptian culture, wise men, sorcerers, and magicians practiced the secret arts. In our culture today, what are some similar examples of practicing the secret arts?

In the cultural category of entertainment, we have numerous examples of books, movies, and shows that are centered on the secret arts (i.e., *The Wizard of Oz, Harry Potter, The Sorcerer's Apprentice*). Are these movies/books just great entertainment or entertainment that softens the serious nature of the dark arts or both? Think about it. Pray about it.

We live as exiles in our culture. We live counter to our culture. We live lives torn, just like Abraham, Isaac, Jacob, Jacob's sons, and Moses.

When it comes to dealing with the dark arts in our culture today . . .

- Describe how your *faith* overrules the *fear* generated by our culture.

- Describe how your *hope* overcomes the *despair* around us.

- Describe how your *love* for God and people overpowers the *hate* that is prevalent in our culture.

## CHAPTER 6

# THE BABYLONIAN EXILE

Before we get to the Babylonian exile, let's set the context by reviewing the key events from the time of Moses to the exile, a span of time that covered about eight hundred years.

After Moses led God's people to the doorstep of the Land of Promise (sadly, after spending 40 years wandering around in the Middle Eastern deserts because of their lack of trust in the Lord God's promises), the Lord God called Joshua to lead his people. This occurred, according to Bible scholars, around the year 1400 B.C.

The Lord God, Yahweh Elohim, was very clear on what he wanted Joshua and his chosen people to do. He wanted them to take total control of the Land of Promise by driving out the hodgepodge of ethnic groups that were occupying the land. Again, sadly, Joshua and the people of Israel failed to complete the total conquest of the land.

As a result, the people often abandoned their worship of Yahweh and started engaging in immoral pagan worship practices. To get the people's attention and to communicate his displeasure with their idolatry and immorality, the Lord God allowed nearby leaders and nations to oppress the people of Israel. Eventually, God's people would cry for help and repent of their idolatry. The Lord would then send a judge (a rescuer or deliverer) to rescue them. For a while, there would be peace in the land. But this cycle of idolatry, oppression, rescue, and peace repeated itself over and over. With every cycle, God's people experienced what it meant to live in exile even though they were living in the Land of Promise.

When the Israelites asked for a king, the Lord God gave them King Saul, who started his reign around 1050 B.C. The reigns of King David and King Solomon followed. Both reigns experienced tremendous blessing from God. After Solomon's reign, however, which ended around 930 B.C., the nation of Israel split into two kingdoms. The northern ten tribes formed the kingdom of Israel, and the two southern tribes formed the kingdom of Judah.

For the kingdom of Israel, the rebellious split ignited a spiritual decline that lasted until 723 B.C. Israel never had a king who was considered faithful to the Lord God during their two hundred-year history as a separate kingdom. In 722 B.C. God allowed the Assyrians to conquer all of Israel, including the capital city of Samaria. The Assyrians took the entire nation captive and dispersed the people into other parts of the Assyrian Empire. The nation of Israel would end its history in exile.

The kingdom of Judah followed the same trajectory as

the kingdom of Israel but at a slower pace of decline. The slower pace was because periodically a faithful king would ascend to the throne who minimized (but never completely eliminated) the pagan idol worship and instead focused the people back on serving the Lord God. But eventually the Lord's patience ran out on Judah's unfaithfulness, idolatry, and wickedness. So he allowed the Babylonians, who had become the dominant world power after defeating the Assyrians in 612 B.C., to invade Judah.

In 605 B.C. King Nebuchadnezzar of Babylon made his first attack on Jerusalem, taking a young man named Daniel, his three companions, and other gifted leaders captive. The captives were sent to Babylon, there to live the rest of their lives in exile. Eight years later, King Nebuchadnezzar attacked Jerusalem a second time. Following this attack, Zedekiah was placed on the throne by Nebuchadnezzar as a puppet king (2 Kings 24–25). Also at this time, a second round of exiles were hauled off to Babylon, including the previous king, Jehoiachin; the queen mother; court officials; other leaders of Judah; and skilled workers and artisans. Zedekiah served as a puppet king in Judah for the next 11 years. Finally in 586 B.C., King Nebuchadnezzar attacked Jerusalem for a final time. This time he burned the temple and destroyed the city. With the city destroyed, the kingdom of Judah went into exile in Babylon five hundred miles away.

Before the final days of his reign, King Zedekiah sent a letter, written by the prophet Jeremiah, to King Nebuchadnezzar. The letter was intended for the leaders of Judah who were already in exile in Babylon. The letter contained specific instructions for how God's people were to live in exile:

> **This is what the Lord Almighty, the God of Israel, says to all those I carried into exile from Jerusalem to Babylon: "Build houses and settle down; plant gardens and eat what they produce. Marry and have sons and daughters; find wives for your sons and give your daughters in marriage, so that they too may have sons and daughters. Increase in number there; do not decrease. Also, seek the peace and prosperity of the city to which I have carried you into exile. Pray to the Lord for it, because if it prospers, you too will prosper."**
>
> **This is what the Lord says: "When seventy years are completed for Babylon, I will come to you and fulfill my good promise to bring you back to this place. For I know the plans I have for you," declares the Lord, "plans to prosper you and not to harm you, plans to give you hope and a future. Then you will call on me and come and pray to me, and I will listen to you. You will seek me and find me when you seek me with all your heart. I will be found by you," declares the Lord, "and will bring you back from captivity. I will gather you from all the nations and places where I have banished you," declares the Lord, "and will bring you back**

**to the place from which I carried you into exile."**
(Jeremiah 29:4–7,10–14)

Before we examine Jeremiah's specific instructions to the exiles, let's take a deeper dive into the word *exile*. For most of my life, I referred to this 70-year period in the kingdom of Judah's history as the Babylonian *captivity*. I assume I was taught that phrase somewhere along the way or read it in a book. But the word *captivity* misses the deeper meaning of the opening sentence of Jeremiah's letter.

Consider this. Who took the people of Jerusalem and Judah captive and led them into captivity in Babylon? It was King Nebuchadnezzar. But that's different than what verse 4 actually says: "This is what the LORD Almighty, the God of Israel, says to all those *I carried into exile* from Jerusalem to Babylon." Who carried the people of Judah into exile? The Lord God did.

The basic meaning of the phrase "carried into exile" (in the Hebrew Bible it's a single word) is "uncover," "reveal," or "remove." The verb form that Jeremiah used, however, adds another dimension to the word. It adds the idea of causing something to happen; i.e., *causing the people to be carried into exile*. And just who caused that? It was the Lord God himself. He caused the people of Jerusalem and Judah to be carried into exile *by* King Nebuchadnezzar. The Babylonian king was just the tool God used to carry out his plan. For the people of Judah, living in exile wasn't their idea. Nor was it Nebuchadnezzar's idea. It was God's idea.

That leads us to a very important truth. *Exile for God's people is never an accident. God chooses exile for his people.*

As mentioned earlier, God's specific instructions to the Babylonian exiles reveal some additional insights into the nature of living in exile while living in the world. Let's enumerate what the Lord God told the exiles to do:

- Build houses.
- Settle down.
- Plant gardens.
- Eat what the gardens produce.
- Get married.
- Have children.
- Find wives for your sons and give your daughters away in marriage.
- Enjoy your grandkids!
- Increase in number.
- Seek the peace and prosperity of the city in which you live.
- Pray that your city prospers.

Put yourself in their shoes for a moment. If you were forced to live as an exile in a foreign country, what would be your attitude, inclinations, and actions? I don't know about you, but for me phrases like "escape exile," "resist the authorities," "oppose the government," "don't cooperate," and "wait it out" come to mind.

But that's the opposite of what the Lord God told them to do. He wanted them to settle down and to settle in, to be hardworking, to get married and have families, to be productive citizens, to pray for prosperity, and to navigate the new culture in which they lived. Those were his directives to his people living in exile.

But what's true for an exile living in a foreign country is also true for Christ followers today living in our *own country*, in our *own culture*. Remember what Jesus prayed for his followers:

> **"I have given them your word and the world has hated them, for they are not of the world any more than I am of the world. My prayer is not that you take them out of the world but that you protect them from the evil one. They are not of the world, even as I am not of it. Sanctify them by the truth; your word is truth."** (John 17:14–17)

No matter where Christ followers live on this planet, they are always living in exile. They live *in* the world but are not *of* the world. That includes you and me.

So whether it was the exiles in Babylon or exiles such as you and me, here's another important truth worth keeping in mind: *Exile isn't a place for waiting or resting. Exile is a place for living, for working, and for prospering.*

In the next chapter, we'll see how Daniel was a great example of this.

## GOD'S TRUTH FOR MY LIFE

Think about what the prophet Jeremiah wrote to the Jewish exiles living in Babylon. What are two or three takeaways for you as you live as an exile in our current culture?

When Ronald Reagan was the governor of the State of California, he gave an inaugural speech in which he spoke about losing freedom:

> "Perhaps you and I have lived too long with this miracle to properly be appreciative. Freedom is a fragile thing, and it's never more than one generation away from extinction. It is not ours by way of inheritance; it must be fought for and defended constantly by each generation, for it comes only once to a people. And those in world history who have known freedom and then lost it have never known it again."[6]

Thinking of the letter that Jeremiah wrote to the exiles in Babylon, on what would Jeremiah and Reagan agree? On what would they disagree?

We live as exiles in our culture. We live counter to our culture. We live lives torn, just like Abraham, Isaac, Jacob, Jacob's sons, Moses, and God's people exiled to Babylon.

When it comes to living as exiles in our own culture . . .

- Describe how your *faith* overrules the *fear* generated by our culture.

- Describe how your *hope* overcomes the *despair* around us.

- Describe how your *love* for God and people overpowers the *hate* that is prevalent in our culture.

# CHAPTER 7

# DANIEL

As we examine the life of Daniel, we'll see some significant similarities between Joseph in Egypt and Daniel in Babylon. Both Joseph and Daniel did not choose to live as exiles in a foreign country. Both rose to positions of high authority after interpreting the dreams of their king, dreams that no one else could explain. Both were faithful to the Lord God and were richly blessed by God for it. Both were a blessing to many others. Both were instruments of God to carry out his plans.

As mentioned in the previous chapter, Daniel and his companions were included in the first round of deportations from Judah to Babylon. So, who was included in that first deportation? Simply put, they were the best and the brightest. King Nebuchadnezzar explained which people he wanted:

> **The king ordered Ashpenaz, chief of his court officials, to bring into the king's service some of the Israelites from the royal family and the nobility—young men without any physical defect, handsome,**

> **showing aptitude for every kind of learning, well informed, quick to understand, and qualified to serve in the king's palace. He was to teach them the language and literature of the Babylonians. The king assigned them a daily amount of food and wine from the king's table. They were to be trained for three years, and after that they were to enter the king's service.** (Daniel 1:3–5)

Four men from Judah were selected—Daniel, Hananiah, Mishael, and Azariah. But the chief official of Nebuchadnezzar gave them new names, Babylonian names, perhaps in a deliberate effort to put some distance between their past and their future. Daniel's new name was Belteshazzar. Hananiah's was Shadrach. Mishael's was Meshach. And Azariah's new name was Abednego.

Living as an exile in a foreign country with its unique culture can create challenges for followers of the Lord God. These four men faced three major changes to their lives when they were deported to Babylon. First, they were required to learn the Babylonian language and literature and train to enter the king's service after three years. This was similar to Moses' training in Egyptian culture. For these four men, this didn't violate their relationship with the Lord. Second, they were given new names, Babylonian names. This too did not violate their relationship with Yahweh. They may not have liked giving up their Hebrew names, but it wasn't a deal-breaker.

But the third change to their lives was a huge challenge. The four were expected to eat and drink from the king's table. Why was that an issue? There were three reasons.

- First, at Mt. Sinai, the Lord God had given dietary restrictions. God's chosen people were only to eat certain foods and were forbidden from eating other foods (such as ham, bacon, shrimp, and lobster—aren't you glad you live in the New Testament era!).
- Second, the meat they ate had to be prepared in a certain way, from how it was butchered to how it was cooked.
- Third, all meals of the Babylonian king had a religious element to them. The king's meal was designed to honor the Babylonian gods with a portion of the meat and wine offered to these gods. Participating in these meals would honor the false gods of the Babylonians. Daniel and his three companions couldn't participate if they wanted to remain faithful to the covenant the Lord established at Mt. Sinai.

So, how did Daniel and his three companions navigate this cultural quandary?

**Daniel resolved not to defile himself with the royal food and wine, and he asked the chief official for permission not to defile himself this way. Now**

**God had caused the official to show favor and compassion to Daniel, but the official told Daniel, "I am afraid of my lord the king, who has assigned your food and drink. Why should he see you looking worse than the other young men your age? The king would then have my head because of you."**

**Daniel then said to the guard whom the chief official had appointed over Daniel, Hananiah, Mishael and Azariah, "Please test your servants for ten days: Give us nothing but vegetables to eat and water to drink. Then compare our appearance with that of the young men who eat the royal food, and treat your servants in accordance with what you see." So he agreed to this and tested them for ten days.**

**At the end of the ten days they looked healthier and better nourished than any of the young men who ate the royal food. So the guard took away their choice food and the wine they were to drink and gave them vegetables instead.** (Daniel 1:8–16)

Two details stand out here. One is that Daniel *asked*. He didn't demand anything of his Babylonian bosses. The second is that the Lord God moved the heart of the chief official to show favor and compassion to Daniel. Daniel's interaction with the chief official reminds us of how we might better approach cultural challenges in our lives. But more important, it reminds us that our God is at work in whatever cultural challenges we face.

The Lord God blessed these four men from Judah in additional ways:

> **To these four young men God gave knowledge and understanding of all kinds of literature and learning. And Daniel could understand visions and dreams of all kinds.**
>
> **At the end of the time set by the king to bring them into his service, the chief official presented them to Nebuchadnezzar. The king talked with them, and he found none equal to Daniel, Hananiah, Mishael and Azariah; so they entered the king's service. In every matter of wisdom and understanding about which the king questioned them, he found them ten times better than all the magicians and enchanters in his whole kingdom.** (Daniel 1:17–20)

Imagine that! The four young men from Judah had ten times the wisdom and understanding when compared to the other "wise men" in Nebuchadnezzar's kingdom. When the Lord God gives his blessing, amazing things happen!

In the second year of his reign, King Nebuchadnezzar experienced some dreams, dreams that troubled him, dreams that disturbed his sleep. But he couldn't remember what the dreams were about, and obviously he didn't know what they meant. So the king sent for his magicians, enchanters, sorcerers, and astrologers to describe his dreams and then to interpret them. This group of soothsayers were more than willing to interpret the dreams if the king would tell them what the dreams were.

Nebuchadnezzar demanded that they tell him what he had dreamed and what the dreams meant. The soothsayers explained that no one could describe the king's dreams, only the king had the ability to do it. The discussion went back and forth until the king got so angry that he ordered the execution of all the wise men in Babylon. On the execution list were Daniel and his three colleagues. Here's what happened next:

> **When Arioch, the commander of the king's guard, had gone out to put to death the wise men of Babylon, Daniel spoke to him with wisdom and tact. He asked the king's officer, "Why did the king issue such a harsh decree?" Arioch then explained the matter to Daniel. At this, Daniel went in to the king and asked for time, so that he might interpret the dream for him.**
>
> **Then Daniel returned to his house and explained the matter to his friends Hananiah, Mishael and Azariah. He urged them to plead for mercy from the God of heaven concerning this mystery, so that he and his friends might not be executed with the rest of the wise men of Babylon. During the night**

> **the mystery was revealed to Daniel in a vision.** (Daniel 2:14–19)

Once again, Daniel spoke with the commander of the king's guard *with wisdom and tact*. Daniel *asked* the king for more time so that he might interpret the dream.

After the Lord God revealed to Daniel in a vision what the king's dream was, Daniel went to Arioch and asked him not to execute the wise men of Babylon because he was now able to tell Nebuchadnezzar what his dream was and what it meant. Together they went to see the king.

The conversation that Daniel had with the king revealed Daniel's heart:

> **The king asked Daniel (also called Belteshazzar), "Are you able to tell me what I saw in my dream and interpret it?"**
>
> **Daniel replied, "No wise man, enchanter, magician or diviner can explain to the king the mystery he has asked about, but there is a God in heaven who reveals mysteries."** (Daniel 2:26–28)

Unlike Arioch, who took credit for finding Daniel, Daniel didn't take credit for the interpretation. He gave the credit to the Lord God in heaven. In the dream that Nebuchadnezzar had, he had seen an enormous, dazzling statue:

> **"The head of the statue was made of pure gold, its chest and arms of silver, its belly and thighs of bronze, its legs of iron, its feet partly of iron and partly of baked clay. While you were watching, a rock was cut out, but not by human hands. It struck the statue on its feet of iron and clay and smashed them. Then the iron, the clay, the bronze, the silver and the gold were all broken to pieces and became like chaff on a threshing floor in the summer. The wind swept them away without leaving a trace. But the rock that struck the statue became a huge mountain and filled the whole earth."** (Daniel 2:32–35)

Daniel went on to explain the meaning of the dream. The four parts of the statue represented four kingdoms. The head of the statue represented Nebuchadnezzar's kingdom, the Babylonian Empire. History tells us that the chest and arms of silver represented the Medo-Persian Empire. The belly and thighs of bronze represented the Greek Empire ruled in the beginning by Alexander the Great. The legs of iron and feet of iron and clay represented the Roman Empire.

But the most significant feature of the dream was the kingdom that would be set up by God himself. It would be a kingdom that lasted forever:

> **"In the time of those kings, the God of heaven will set up a kingdom that will never be destroyed, nor**

> **will it be left to another people. It will crush all those kingdoms and bring them to an end, but it will itself endure forever. This is the meaning of the vision of the rock cut out of a mountain, but not by human hands—a rock that broke the iron, the bronze, the clay, the silver and the gold to pieces."** (Daniel 2:44,45)

God's Son came to this earth during the time of the Roman Empire. With Jesus' life, death, and resurrection, he established his kingdom. It's Christ's church, the gathering of all who put their faith in Jesus. This kingdom will outlast any earthly kingdom. Jesus promised that even **"the gates of Hades will not overcome it"** (Matthew 16:18).

But there is more to this kingdom. When Jesus returns on the Last Day, all the nations of the world will be destroyed and Jesus will rule over his kingdom. That's what the apostle John saw and heard in his vision recorded in the book of Revelation: **"The seventh angel sounded his trumpet, and there were loud voices in heaven, which said: 'The kingdom of the world has become the kingdom of our Lord and of his Messiah, and he will reign for ever and ever'"** (11:15).

Daniel finished his interpretation of Nebuchadnezzar's dream by once again giving credit where credit was due: **"The great God has shown the king what will take place in the future. The dream is true and its interpretation is trustworthy"** (Daniel 2:45). Nebuchadnezzar was the first king to whom Daniel witnessed his faith in the true God of heaven and earth.

King Nebuchadnezzar had promised that whoever could interpret his dream would be rewarded greatly—gifts, rewards, and great honor. The king kept his promise. The king gave Daniel many gifts, made him ruler over the entire province of Babylon, and put him in charge of all its wise men.

Almost all of the Old Testament was written in Hebrew, the Semitic language of the people of Israel, the Jews. The other language of the Old Testament is Aramaic. Aramaic is also from the family of Semitic languages. It was the language of the Babylonian Empire. It was also the language used in commerce and diplomacy. It was more of a universal language, much as English is today in our world.

Two books in the Old Testament have longer sections written in Aramaic, Daniel and Ezra. Daniel 2:4 through the end of chapter 7 is written in Aramaic. The rest of the book is written in Hebrew.

Not surprisingly, Daniel authored the book of Daniel. There are references in the book itself that point to Daniel as the author even though there is no heading or direct reference to him being the author. However, in Matthew chapter 24, Jesus quotes from the book of Daniel and refers to Daniel as the author. But there is another author in the book in chapter 4. It is King Nebuchadnezzar himself.

In between Daniel chapter 2, where Daniel interpreted the king's dream about the statue, and chapter 4, which records the words of Nebuchadnezzar, is the account of the three men in the fiery furnace. Shadrach, Meshach, and Abednego were thrown into a furnace of fire for failing to bow down to King Nebuchadnezzar's 90-foot image of gold.

The three men were thrown into the fire. When Nebuchadnezzar looked into the fire, he saw four men in the fire walking around unharmed. The king called them out of the fire. They were unharmed, unsinged, and didn't even smell of smoke. Nebuchadnezzar's reaction was priceless:

> **"Praise be to the God of Shadrach, Meshach and Abednego, who has sent his angel and rescued his servants! They trusted in him and defied the king's command and were willing to give up their lives rather than serve or worship any god except their own God. Therefore I decree that the people of any nation or language who say anything against the God of Shadrach, Meshach and Abednego be cut into pieces and their houses be turned into piles of rubble, for no other god can save in this way."**
>
> **Then the king promoted Shadrach, Meshach and Abednego in the province of Babylon.** (Daniel 3:28-30)

As Daniel did, Shadrach, Meshach, and Abednego had an opportunity to witness their faith in the true God of heaven and earth.

The fiery furnace event is followed by King

Nebuchadnezzar's message, in Aramaic, to the world, recorded in chapter 4:

> **King Nebuchadnezzar,**
>
> **To the nations and peoples of every language, who live in all the earth: May you prosper greatly!**
>
> **It is my pleasure to tell you about the miraculous signs and wonders that the Most High God has performed for me.**
>
> **How great are his signs, how mighty his wonders! His kingdom is an eternal kingdom; his dominion endures from generation to generation.** (Daniel 4:1–3)

Just think of it—a pagan king from a pagan nation writing to the pagan world. It happened because of how the Lord God gifted Daniel, Shadrach, Meshach, and Abednego to accomplish his purposes.

In his message to the world, Nebuchadnezzar then recounted another dream that he had experienced, a dream interpreted again by Daniel. This dream and its fulfillment would dramatically affect Nebuchadnezzar's remaining reign.

This dream was about an enormous tree with leaves and fruit, birds perching in the tree, and animals being fed from the fruit of the tree. Then a holy one from heaven called for the tree to be cut down, leaving just the stump and roots.

Then there is a reference to an unknown person: **"Let him be drenched with the dew of heaven, and let him live with the animals among the plants of the earth. Let his mind be changed from that of a man and let him be given the mind of an animal, till seven times pass by for him"** (Daniel 4:15,16). This was Nebuchadnezzar's dream.

The king ordered that all the wise men of Babylon be brought in to interpret the dream. None of them could. So the king summoned Daniel. After Daniel heard the details of the dream, he was reluctant to tell the king what it meant. Finally, with assurances from the king, Daniel explained the dream. The tree and the person in the dream were King Nebuchadnezzar, and what happened to that tree and person would be Nebuchadnezzar's future:

> **"This is the interpretation, Your Majesty, and this is the decree the Most High has issued against my lord the king: You will be driven away from people and will live with the wild animals; you will eat grass like the ox and be drenched with the dew of heaven. Seven times will pass by for you until you acknowledge that the Most High is sovereign over all kingdoms on earth and gives them to anyone he wishes. The command to leave the stump of the tree with its roots means that your kingdom will be restored to you when you acknowledge that Heaven rules. Therefore, Your Majesty, be pleased to accept my advice: Renounce your sins by doing**

**what is right, and your wickedness by being kind to the oppressed. It may be that then your prosperity will continue."**

**All this happened to King Nebuchadnezzar. Twelve months later, as the king was walking on the roof of the royal palace of Babylon, he said, "Is not this the great Babylon I have built as the royal residence, by my mighty power and for the glory of my majesty?"**

**Even as the words were on his lips, a voice came from heaven, "This is what is decreed for you, King Nebuchadnezzar: Your royal authority has been taken from you. You will be driven away from people and will live with the wild animals; you will eat grass like the ox. Seven times will pass by for you until you acknowledge that the Most High is sovereign over all kingdoms on earth and gives them to anyone he wishes."** (Daniel 4:24–32)

Everything Daniel said would happen to the king did. The king experienced a period of insanity and was driven away from his people. He lived in the wild like an animal until his sanity was restored. After he regained his mental capacity, he gave honor and glory to the God of heaven and earth:

**His dominion is an eternal dominion; his kingdom endures from generation to generation. All the peoples of the earth are regarded as nothing. He does as he pleases with the powers of heaven and the peoples of the earth. No one can hold back his hand or say to him: "What have you done?"** (Daniel 4:34,35)

The king's advisors and nobles sought out Nebuchadnezzar and restored him to his throne. In the last words we have from the king, Nebuchadnezzar acknowledged that the King of heaven was right and just and that he can humble any ruler filled with pride. Nebuchadnezzar knew that from firsthand experience.

Man-made kingdoms rise and fall. They rise and fall because the King of heaven is in control of all things. Because of that, we ought not question what the Lord God does or why. Instead we acknowledge his sovereignty and find comfort in the fact that he does all things for the good of his kingdom.

After Nebuchadnezzar's reign ended, a ruler by the name of Belshazzar succeeded him on Babylon's throne. The only thing that the Bible tells us about Belshazzar is that he hosted a great banquet for a thousand of his nobles. This banquet was more than a social event. It had a religious aspect to it. That's because Belshazzar ordered that the gold and silver goblets that had been taken from the temple in Jerusalem by Nebuchadnezzar be brought to the banquet and used by the guests. **"As they drank the wine, they**

**praised the gods of gold and silver, of bronze, iron, wood and stone"** (Daniel 5:4). In praising the Babylonians' gods with goblets taken from Yahweh's temple, they were also ridiculing the Lord God who claimed to be the one true God.

Suddenly, the fingers of a human hand began to write words on a wall in the royal palace, and Belshazzar watched. He didn't know what the words were or what they meant, so he called for his enchanters, astrologers, and diviners. When the Babylonian wise men couldn't decipher the words, the queen reminded Belshazzar of a man who could—Daniel.

When Daniel was brought before the king, he reminded Belshazzar what had happened to Nebuchadnezzar because of his arrogance. Daniel reminded Belshazzar that the former king was given the mind of an animal until he acknowledged that the Most High God is sovereign over the kingdoms of men. Then Daniel told Belshazzar:

> **"But you, Belshazzar, his son, have not humbled yourself, though you knew all this. Instead, you have set yourself up against the Lord of heaven. You had the goblets from his temple brought to you, and you and your nobles, your wives and your concubines drank wine from them. You praised the gods of silver and gold, of bronze, iron, wood and stone, which cannot see or hear or understand. But you did not honor the God who holds in his hand your life and all your ways. Therefore he sent the hand that wrote the inscription.**

**"This is the inscription that was written:**

> **MENE, MENE, TEKEL, PARSIN**

**"Here is what these words mean:**

> ***Mene*: God has numbered the days of your reign and brought it to an end.**
> ***Tekel*: You have been weighed on the scales and found wanting.**
> ***Peres*: Your kingdom is divided and given to the Medes and Persians."**

**Then at Belshazzar's command, Daniel was clothed in purple, a gold chain was placed around his neck, and he was proclaimed the third highest ruler in the kingdom.**

**That very night Belshazzar, king of the Babylonians, was slain, and Darius the Mede took over the kingdom, at the age of sixty-two.** (Daniel 5:22–30)

Belshazzar was the second king to whom Daniel witnessed his faith in the true God of heaven and earth.

In 539 B.C. Cyrus the Great conquered Babylon and expanded the Medo-Persian Empire to include the former Babylonian Empire. Cyrus was the ruler of this expansive kingdom and would rule for an additional nine years. In addition, it was Cyrus, in the first year of his reign, who decreed that any Jewish exile in Babylon could return to Jerusalem to help rebuild the temple. Cyrus even sent along 5,400 articles of gold and silver that Nebuchadnezzar had taken from Solomon's temple 70 years earlier.

So, who is Darius the Mede? That's an interesting question. The person known as Darius who conquered Babylon is only mentioned in the Bible. Bible scholars have offered several explanations. Some have suggested that Darius was another name for Gobryas, whom Cyrus had appointed as governor over Babylon when the city fell. Others have suggested that Darius was a title of authority. Historians aren't absolutely certain about the identity of Darius.

However, it seems that the most plausible explanation is that Cyrus and Darius were the same person because . . .

- Daniel 6:28 can be translated one of two ways: **"So Daniel prospered during the reign of Darius and the reign of Cyrus the Persian."** Or, **"So Daniel prospered during the reign of Darius, that is, the reign of Cyrus the Persian."**
- Through his mother, Cyrus was a royal descendant of the Median kingdom. Through his father, Cyrus was in line to inherit the Persian throne. The two names emphasize both the Median and Persian royal lines.
- The name Darius was used as the royal name for three of Cyrus' successors.

- The Greek historian Herodotus wrote that Cyrus was not the original name given to him by his Median mother.
- When Babylon fell, Cyrus was 62 years old. When Babylon fell, Darius was 62 years old. Coincidence?
- Daniel knew Darius personally, served under him, and referred to him by that name.

Is there absolute evidence that Cyrus and Darius were one and the same? No. But is there circumstantial evidence? Yes.

Under Darius, **"Daniel so distinguished himself among the administrators and the satraps by his exceptional qualities that the king planned to set him over the whole kingdom"** (Daniel 6:3). That, however, didn't sit well with the other officials, especially since Daniel was an exile from Judah. So they concocted a plan and convinced Darius to sign their plan into law, a law that could not be annulled. The enemies of Daniel convinced Darius that if anyone in the following 30 days prayed to a god or man other than Darius, that person would be fed to the lions.

**"Now when Daniel learned that the decree had been published, he went home to his upstairs room where the windows opened toward Jerusalem. Three times a day he got down on his knees and prayed, giving thanks to his God, just as he had done before"** (Daniel 6:10). This was one of Daniel's *nonnegotiables*. To remain faithful to the Lord

God, Daniel needed to ignore the king's edict. And Daniel made no attempt to hide his prayers. It was a public confession of whom he worshiped.

Because he violated the king's edict, Daniel was arrested and, with much regret, the king gave the order to have Daniel thrown into a lions' den.

> **At the first light of dawn, the king got up and hurried to the lions' den. When he came near the den, he called to Daniel in an anguished voice, "Daniel, servant of the living God, has your God, whom you serve continually, been able to rescue you from the lions?"**
>
> **Daniel answered, "May the king live forever! My God sent his angel, and he shut the mouths of the lions. They have not hurt me, because I was found innocent in his sight. Nor have I ever done any wrong before you, Your Majesty."** (Daniel 6:19–22)

There were two outcomes to Daniel's miraculous deliverance. The first was that Darius ordered all those who plotted Daniel's demise to suffer what they had planned for Daniel. They were thrown to the lions. The second outcome was that Darius delivered a message to the world:

> **Then King Darius wrote to all the nations and peoples of every language in all the earth:**

**"May you prosper greatly!**

**"I issue a decree that in every part of my kingdom people must fear and reverence the God of Daniel.**

**"For he is the living God**
 **and he endures forever;**
**his kingdom will not be destroyed,**
 **his dominion will never end.**
**He rescues and he saves;**
 **he performs signs and wonders**
 **in the heavens and on the earth.**
**He has rescued Daniel**
 **from the power of the lions."**

**So Daniel prospered during the reign of Darius and** (that is) **the reign of Cyrus the Persian.** (Daniel 6:25–28)

Darius was the third king to whom Daniel witnessed his faith in the true God of heaven and earth.

Daniel is one of the best examples of a follower of the true God living as an exile while living in the world. Not only did he live as an exile in a foreign land for most of his life; he also lived as an exile in the Babylonian culture. Daniel was a man of integrity. His honesty and loyalty resulted in his Babylonian bosses rewarding him with position and authority.

Yet through it all, he never wavered in his faith and his relationship with the Lord. And because of it, the Lord God chose to bless him. Daniel's exile reminds us that *exile for God's people is never an accident. God chooses exile for his people in order to carry out his plans and purposes.*

## GOD'S TRUTH FOR MY LIFE

List Daniel's attitudes and personal qualities that allowed him to enjoy the favor of his Babylonian bosses.

Throughout Daniel's life, we learn about a couple of his non-negotiables when it came to his relationship with his God. Nonnegotiables are what believers are willing to die for.

- What were the two examples of Daniel's nonnegotiables that you observed?
- What are two or three nonnegotiables in your relationship with your God and Savior Jesus for which you would be willing to die?

We live as exiles in our culture. We live counter to our culture. We live lives torn, just like Abraham, Isaac, Jacob, Jacob's sons, Moses, God's people exiled to Babylon, and Daniel.

When it comes to holding on to and practicing our nonnegotiables . . .

- Describe how your *faith* overrules the *fear* generated by our culture.

- Describe how your *hope* overcomes the *despair* around us.

- Describe how your *love* for God and people overpowers the *hate* that is prevalent in our culture.

# CHAPTER 8

# ESTHER

As we explore the story of Esther's life and service to God's Old Testament people, we observe some similarities to Daniel's life. Some of Daniel's qualities that endeared him to both his Babylonian and Persian bosses were humility and the showing of honor and respect. The same was true of Esther.

Esther's story is also much like the story of Joseph. Both Joseph and Esther lived under rulers who had control over the Jewish people. In both of their lives, we observe the Lord God charting a course that enabled his plans for his people to be accomplished. As the Lord's plans unfolded, both Esther and Joseph demonstrated wisdom and courage to help God's people.

Esther lived at the time of a Persian king, who in the Hebrew Bible has the Hebrew name Ahasuerus. So, what was his Persian name? He was the Persian king Xerxes. Xerxes I ruled the Persian Empire from 485 to 465 B.C. Many English Bible translations simply transliterate the Hebrew word into English. Other English translations substitute Ahasuerus with the historical name of the Persian king—Xerxes.

To be transparent, there are some Bible scholars and historians who claim that Esther lived at a later time, either at the time of Artaxerxes I (465–424 B.C.) or Artaxerxes II (404–358 B.C.). The Greek historian Herodotus, however, seems to settle the matter. He wrote extensively about the Persian kings and the Persian wars. You see, Herodotus was born in 484 B.C. and lived during the reign of the father/son rulers, Xerxes I and Artaxerxes I. He indicated in his writings that Ahasuerus was, in fact, Xerxes I, a king rich and powerful yet lacking good judgment and common sense.

From the perspective of her fellow exiles, Esther lived *after* the time when the first exiles had returned to Jerusalem to rebuild the temple under the leadership of Zerubbabel (Ezra 6) but *before* the time when Ezra (Ezra 7), the Jewish scribe and priest, returned. Between chapters 6 and 7 of the book of Ezra, there is a gap of about 50 years. In that gap is where we find the story of Esther.

In the opening chapter of the book of Esther, we learn that King Xerxes ruled over 127 provinces from India to what today is the country of Ethiopia, located southeast of Egypt and Sudan, on the continent of Africa. In the third year of his reign, Xerxes gave a weeklong banquet for the princes and nobles from the 127 provinces.

King Xerxes had a queen. Her name was Vashti. At the same time that Xerxes gave a banquet for the princes and nobles, Vashti gave a banquet for the women, presumably the women who accompanied the princes and nobles. On day seven of the banquet, Xerxes, who was **"in high spirits from wine"** (Esther 1:10), commanded his servants to bring his beautiful queen, Vashti, to his banquet wearing her crown (apparently only her crown). Vashti refused. The king became furious over what he considered Vashti's disrespect and disobedience. He consulted with his advisors on how to handle the situation. The end result was that Queen Vashti was deposed, never to set foot in the palace again.

It's tempting to focus on the moral failures of Xerxes and Vashti, but that's not the point of the biblical account. The Bible tells us about the breakup of Xerxes and Vashti because it was the way the Lord God directed human events to open up the opportunity for Esther to become queen. You see, the king's advisors had also suggested that Queen Vashti be replaced with someone better. Xerxes' personal attendants suggested that a search be made throughout the entire kingdom to find potential candidates, one of whom would be the next queen.

Meet Mordecai, an exile who lived in the capital city of Susa. He had been exiled to Babylon by King Nebuchadnezzar and served in some capacity in the king's court. Mordecai had a cousin named Hadassah, whose Persian name was Esther. The name Esther meant "star" and perhaps was derived from the heathen goddess' name, Ishtar. Because Esther's parents had died, Mordecai took Esther under his wing and watched out for her.

Esther, because she was a virgin and very beautiful, was selected as one of the candidates for queen. It is likely that

Esther had no say in the matter, although the Bible doesn't say. All the candidates were brought to the palace and placed under the care of Hegai, one of the king's eunuchs, who was in charge of the harem.

It is at this point that we see the hand of God influencing Hegai's attitude and actions toward Esther:

> **She pleased him and won his favor. Immediately he provided her with her beauty treatments and special food. He assigned to her seven female attendants selected from the king's palace and moved her and her attendants into the best place in the harem.** (Esther 2:9)

Mordecai encouraged Esther not to reveal that she was Jewish. She followed his advice.

What happened next strains at our understanding of God's gift of sex and marriage and doesn't fit at all with our cultural perspective. But it was the way ancient kings in their cultures selected a queen:

> **Before a young woman's turn came to go in to King Xerxes, she had to complete twelve months of beauty treatments prescribed for the women, six months with oil of myrrh and six with perfumes and cosmetics. And this is how she would go to the king: Anything she wanted was given her to take with her from the harem to the king's palace. In**

**the evening she would go there and in the morning return to another part of the harem to the care of Shaashgaz, the king's eunuch who was in charge of the concubines. She would not return to the king unless he was pleased with her and summoned her by name.**

**When the turn came for Esther (the young woman Mordecai had adopted, the daughter of his uncle Abihail) to go to the king, she asked for nothing other than what Hegai, the king's eunuch who was in charge of the harem, suggested. And Esther won the favor of everyone who saw her. She was taken to King Xerxes in the royal residence in the tenth month, the month of Tebeth, in the seventh year of his reign.**

**Now the king was attracted to Esther more than to any of the other women, and she won his favor and approval more than any of the other virgins. So he set a royal crown on her head and made her queen instead of Vashti. And the king gave a great banquet, Esther's banquet, for all his nobles and officials. He proclaimed a holiday throughout the provinces and distributed gifts with royal liberality.** (2:12–18)

The king chose Esther to be his queen.

After Esther became queen, we learn of an event involving Mordecai. One day Mordecai overheard two of the king's officers conspiring to assassinate Xerxes. Mordecai reported this to Esther, and Esther reported it to the king, giving credit to Mordecai for the information. More on this later.

King Xerxes may have chosen Esther to be his queen but, behind the scenes, it was the Lord God who led the king to choose Esther as his queen. As queen, Esther would be key to carrying out God's plan to save his people.

Meet Haman, a Persian noble. We're not told why, but the king elevated Haman to a new position and gave him a seat of honor higher than any other noble. The king instructed his royal officials to bow to Haman whenever he was in their presence. All the royal officials did as the king commanded except for one, Mordecai. This angered Haman, so much so that he planned to kill Mordecai. But after learning that Mordecai was a Jew, he decided not only to kill Mordecai but all of Mordecai's people.

Haman's plan was to disparage the Jewish people before the king (without naming them) and suggested they be eliminated:

> **Then Haman said to King Xerxes, "There is a certain people dispersed among the peoples in all the provinces of your kingdom who keep themselves separate. Their customs are different from those of all other people, and they do not obey the king's laws; it is not in the king's best**

**interest to tolerate them. If it pleases the king, let a decree be issued to destroy them, and I will give ten thousand talents of silver to the king's administrators for the royal treasury."**

**So the king took his signet ring from his finger and gave it to Haman son of Hammedatha, the Agagite, the enemy of the Jews. "Keep the money," the king said to Haman, "and do with the people as you please."**

**Dispatches were sent by couriers to all the king's provinces with the order to destroy, kill and annihilate all the Jews—young and old, women and children—on a single day, the thirteenth day of the twelfth month, the month of Adar, and to plunder their goods.** (3:8-11,13)

To determine by lottery the exact day that this decree would be carried out—a *pur,* that is—a lot was cast by the royal officials in the presence of Haman. The pur fell to the 13th day of the 12th month.

When Mordecai learned of the king's decree, he tore his clothes and put on sackcloth and ashes. He was joined by other Jews who walked the streets of the city weeping and wailing. When Esther learned that Mordecai was in sackcloth and ashes, she sent clothes to him, but he refused to wear them. Then she sent one of the king's eunuchs to find out what was troubling Mordecai. Mordecai gave a copy of the edict for their annihilation to the eunuch with instructions that Esther read it. He also told the eunuch to encourage Esther to go into the king's presence and beg for mercy.

Esther was reluctant to approach the king. She explained why in her message back to Mordecai: **"All the king's officials and the people of the royal provinces know that for any man or woman who approaches the king in the inner court without being summoned the king has but one law: that they be put to death unless the king extends the gold scepter to them and spares their lives. But thirty days have passed since I was called to go to the king"** (4:11).

Mordecai's response to Esther's hesitancy was compelling:

> **"Do not think that because you are in the king's house you alone of all the Jews will escape. For if you remain silent at this time, relief and deliverance for the Jews will arise from another place, but you and your father's family will perish. And who knows but that you have come to your royal position for such a time as this?"** (4:13,14)

Mordecai expressed the fear that Esther's silence would end with her death and his own death. Yet Mordecai also expressed a confident faith that even if Esther would remain silent, the Lord God would provide deliverance for the Jewish people from another place.

Then Mordecai expressed what is actually the theme of the book: *"And who knows but that you have come to your royal position for such a time as this?"* Although Mordecai (and Esther too) may not have realized why Esther had become queen, it was starting to dawn on Mordecai that the Lord God had been working behind the scenes *for such a time as this*.

Esther agreed to go to the king. Before she did, however, she asked that all the Jews living in the capital city of Susa join her in fasting for three days. **"When this is done, I will go to the king, even though it is against the law. And if I perish, I perish"** (4:16).

After three days of fasting, Esther put on her royal robes and stood in the inner court of the palace in front of the king's hall. When the king saw Esther, he was pleased and extended his gold scepter.

> **Then the king asked, "What is it, Queen Esther? What is your request? Even up to half the kingdom, it will be given you."**
>
> **"If it pleases the king," replied Esther, "let the king, together with Haman, come today to a banquet I have prepared for him."**
>
> **"Bring Haman at once," the king said, "so that we may do what Esther asks."** (5:3–5)

At the banquet, the king asked Esther once again what her request was. He was willing to give her up to half of his kingdom. For whatever reason, Esther hesitated. Had she lost her nerve? Did she sense this wasn't the best time? Was there some other reason? We don't know. Instead, she invited the king and Haman to a second banquet to be held the next day.

This was a great day for Haman, at least until he saw Mordecai at the king's gate and observed that Mordecai didn't rise to honor him. Because of Mordecai's insolence, Haman was filled with rage and went to tell his wife and his friends both about it being a great day with a potentially better day to come, as well as dissatisfaction because of that Jew Mordecai. Both his wife and his friends suggested that he have a gallows built and then ask the king the following morning to have Mordecai hanged on it.

When we think of a gallows, we typically think of a structure from which a person is hanged with a rope. The following verses give us a different picture. Haman was intending to ask the king permission to impale Mordecai on the pole he had constructed. The Greek historian Herodotus, whom I mentioned earlier, indicated in his writings that impalement was a Persian form of capital punishment.

We observe the hand of God's providence once again. That night, it just so happened that the king couldn't sleep. He had insomnia. So he ordered the record of his reign be brought in and read to him. It just so happened that one of the records in the book that was read to the king indicated that Mordecai had uncovered an assassination plot. The king asked:

> **"What honor and recognition has Mordecai received for this?" the king asked.**
>
> **"Nothing has been done for him," his attendants answered.**
>
> **The king said, "Who is in the court?" Now Haman had just entered the outer court of the palace to speak to the king about impaling Mordecai on the pole he had set up for him.**
>
> **His attendants answered, "Haman is standing in the court."**
>
> **"Bring him in," the king ordered.**
>
> **When Haman entered, the king asked him, "What should be done for the man the king delights to honor?"** (6:3-6)

When the king asked what should be done for a man whom the king wants to honor, Haman immediately thought that the king wanted to honor him. So he shared a rather self-serving list:

- Have the man wear a robe that the king has previously worn.
- Have the man ride a horse that the king has previously ridden.
- Have the man and horse entrusted to one of the king's most noble princes.
- Have the prince lead the man on the horse through the city streets proclaiming to the people, "This is what is done for the man the king wants to honor."

Imagine Haman's surprise when the king told him, "You, Haman, go and get Mordecai. Put a robe on him and lead him on horseback through the city streets proclaiming, 'This is what is done for the man the king wants to honor.'"

After the parade through the streets, Haman went home filled with grief and told his wife and friends all that had happened. While they were talking, the king's eunuchs arrived at his house to take him to the banquet that Esther had prepared for the king and Haman.

At the banquet given by Esther, the king asked once again what he could do for her, up to half of his kingdom. Esther replied:

> **"If I have found favor with you, Your Majesty, and if it pleases you, grant me my life—this is my petition. And spare my people—this is my request. For I and my people have been sold to be destroyed,**

**killed and annihilated. If we had merely been sold as male and female slaves, I would have kept quiet, because no such distress would justify disturbing the king."**

**King Xerxes asked Queen Esther, "Who is he? Where is he—the man who has dared to do such a thing?"**

**Esther said, "An adversary and enemy! This vile Haman!"** (7:3–6)

Haman's doom was now sealed. Instead of Mordecai being impaled on Haman's pole, Haman was. The wealthy estate of Haman was given to Queen Esther because he had attacked the Jews. Esther then told the king about Mordecai and their family relationship. The king appointed Mordecai to the position that Haman previously had and gave the signet ring also to Mordecai, which Haman had originally worn.

But there was still a problem. The royal decree authorizing the annihilation of the Jewish people was still in effect. In Persian culture, once a royal decree was published, it could not be rescinded. The only way to address this problem was to issue a second decree to minimize the impact of the first decree.

Esther used the king's favor for her to get this second decree drafted. Mordecai offered guidance to the king and oversaw the distribution of the second decree across the vast empire. This second decree stated that the Jewish people could use the same methods and activities that were outlined in the first decree. Haman's decree had stated, **"Kill and annihilate all the Jews—young and old, women and children—on a single day, the thirteenth day of the twelfth month, the month of Adar, and to plunder their goods"** (3:13). The Jewish people and the enemies of the Jewish people would now be on a level playing field. And they had ten months to prepare for it.

When that fateful day, determined by the casting of the pur, arrived, the Jewish people were prepared. They acted both offensively and defensively in taking on their enemies who were seeking to annihilate them. At the end of the day, God's people were saved. And why? It was because the Lord stepped in to preserve his people and fulfill his promises.

Esther was a Jewish exile living in the Persian Empire. She was torn between saving her own life or her own people when she first approached the king without an invitation. She was torn again when she risked her own life to address the king with Haman's genocidal edict. Esther navigated the Persian culture to serve her people. And the Lord God blessed it.

There are two main takeaways from Esther's story. First of all, Mordecai was right. **"And who knows but that you have come to your royal position for such a time as this?"** (4:14). The Lord God placed Esther in her position as queen to save his people.

Second, no matter what happens in your personal life, the life of those you love, and the culture in which we all live, *God's got this.* He is sovereign. We will be delivered from evil. His kingdom will come. His will always will be done on earth and in heaven. That's because he loves us. When we think about God's love for us, who could say it better than the apostle Paul in his letter to the Christians living in Rome: **"In all these things we are more than conquerors through him who loved us. For I am convinced that neither death nor life, neither angels nor demons, neither the present nor the future, nor any powers, neither height nor depth, nor anything else in all creation, will be able to separate us from the love of God that is in Christ Jesus our Lord"** (Romans 8:37–39).

## GOD'S TRUTH FOR MY LIFE

Haman, along with tens of thousands of people within the Persian Empire, hated God's Old Testament chosen people. The hatred was so intense against the Jews that they sought to annihilate them, to commit genocide.

- What other examples from history can you point to where the Jewish people were targeted specifically for annihilation?

- Give one or two examples of how the Jewish people are still hated today.

- Give one or two examples of how Christians are hated today.

Is it God's providence or coincidence? One of the key themes of Esther's life is that our God shapes the future by stepping in to the present to ensure that his will is done and his promises fulfilled.

- Identify from the life of Esther all the times the Lord God stepped in to the present to influence the future.

- In your life (or the life of someone you know), can you point to an event that others might call "coincidence" but that you believe was the hand of God?

We live as exiles in our culture. We live counter to our culture. We live lives torn, just like Abraham, Isaac, Jacob, Jacob's sons, Moses, God's people exiled to Babylon, Daniel, and Esther.

When it comes to trusting that *God's got this* as we live as exiles in our culture . . .

- Describe how your *faith* overrules the *fear* generated by our culture.

- Describe how your *hope* overcomes the *despair* around us.

- Describe how your *love* for God and people overpowers the *hate* that is prevalent in our culture.

## CHAPTER 9

# CHRISTIANITY IN THE FIRST THREE CENTURIES A.D.

In chapter 1 we observed that one of the key reasons why Christ followers living in the first century became exiles was because of real-life persecution. That real-life persecution would continue into the second and third centuries as well. We're not talking about criticism or ridicule or marginalization or even ostracism for being a Christian. We're talking about dying for one's confession of Christ. Let's dig into the past a bit more to understand what it meant to live as an exile in the culture of the New Testament world.

First, let's understand the demographics of the people living in the first centuries after Jesus' ascension. But we need to do so with a disclaimer. In doing research about the first few centuries, one discovers quickly that there is a wide range of thought when it comes to such things as the population in the world, the number or percentage of Christ followers who lived in the world, and the number of Christ followers who lost their lives because of their confession of

Christ. The numbers that follow are just estimates based upon reasoned assumptions. And it's understandable why they are only estimates. Demographic tracking in the first few centuries wasn't a priority or a practiced skill as it is today.

It's generally believed among Bible scholars that Jesus completed his three-year ministry around the year A.D. 30. By A.D. 100, all the missionary journeys of the apostle Paul and the other apostles were completed. Also by A.D. 100, all the books of the New Testament had been written.

Historians estimate that at the end of the first century, the total population in the world was between 60 million and 100 million people (an example of a *wide range*). Of those, historians estimate that there were less than 10,000 people who called themselves Christians. That number was a tiny percentage of the world's population. To illustrate that, it would mean that in a city with a population of 10,000, there would be fewer than 2 Christians, no matter whether there were 60 million or 100 million in the total population pool.

After A.D. 100, Christianity soon began to experience growth in numbers. By A.D. 150, historians project that there were between 40,000 and 50,000 people who claimed a faith in Jesus Christ. By A.D. 200, that number had increased to 200,000. By A.D. 300, it had ballooned into the millions, with estimates ranging from 3 to 6 million (another example of a *wide range*).

What's remarkable is that this exponential growth occurred during three centuries when followers of Christ experienced periods of persecution by the Roman government. If you know about the Roman's attitude toward other religious groups, that might seem a bit odd. Although the Romans typically embraced the gods and goddesses of the countries they had conquered, the Christian God wasn't one of them. Get this. Christians weren't even considered *religious.* Christians were tagged as *atheists* because they didn't acknowledge or honor the Roman gods. And the penalty for being an *atheist* often meant an automatic death sentence.

Persecution of Christians, however, didn't start with the Romans. It started with the Jews. With the stoning of Stephen (Acts 7) by a Jerusalem mob, the pre-conversion persecution of Saul (Acts 9), and the execution of James—one of Jesus' disciples—by King Herod Agrippa in order to please the Jews (Acts 12), the persecution of Christians by the Jews became a tenacious practice. During the three decades following Jesus' life, death, and resurrection, the Roman authorities never saw Christians as a serious threat, but the Jews did.

That changed however in A.D. 64. On July 19 of that year, there was a massive fire that engulfed much of the city of Rome. Of the 14 quarters of the city, 10 experienced damage from the fire. The Roman emperor at that time was Nero. The people of the city surmised that Nero had set the fires himself either for his own amusement or to create new vacant land for his massive building projects. Nero wanted to squelch that kind of talk.

To change the narrative, Nero first blamed the Jews, who had a reputation for arson activity as part of their rebellion playbook against the Roman government. But then Nero shifted the blame to the Christians. Many Christians in Rome were subsequently put to death. The following account was written by the Roman historian Tacitus, who had lived as a young lad during Nero's persecution of Christians:

> Therefore, to stop the rumor [that he had set Rome on fire], he [Emperor Nero] falsely charged with guilt, and punished with the most fearful tortures, the persons commonly called Christians, who were [generally] hated for their enormities.
>
> Christus, the founder of that name, was put to death as a criminal by Pontius Pilate, procurator of Judea, in the reign of Tiberius, but the pernicious superstition—repressed for a time, broke out yet again, not only through Judea—where mischief originated, but through the city of Rome also, whither all things horrible and disgraceful flow from all quarters, as to a common receptacle, and where they are encouraged. Accordingly first those were arrested who confessed they were Christians; next on their information, a vast multitude were convicted, not so much on the charge of burning the city, as of "hating the human race."
>
> In their very deaths they were made the subjects of sport: for they were covered with the hides of

> wild beasts, and worried to death by dogs, or nailed to crosses, or set fire to, and when the day waned, burned to serve for the evening lights.[7]

As Tacitus' account revealed, Nero was a brutal tyrant. Some historians, specifically Origen and Eusebius, indicated that both the apostle Peter and the apostle Paul, along with other New Testament Christian leaders, were martyred at the hands of Nero.

In the New Testament world, Christians were losing their lives.

The persecution of Christians was intermittent for the first three centuries. This wasn't a nonstop persecution of Christians as one might think. After Nero, three decades passed before a second round of Christian persecutions was initiated by another Roman emperor. That emperor was Domitian. His reign was relatively brief. He ruled from A.D. 89 to 96.

Domitian had a reputation for being cruel, both to the members of his own family but especially to the members of the Roman Senate. Domitian thought that he should rule Rome autonomously, so he greatly diminished the power of the senate. He even had some senators executed, either out of malice or because Domitian wanted their land holdings for himself. He was a reckless ruler who undermined his own people.

According to some historians, both secular and church historians, Jews and Christians were persecuted toward the end of Domitian's reign. There is, however, no consensus as to the scope and frequency of these persecutions. The book of Revelation was written by the apostle John during the reign of Domitian, who banished John to the island of Patmos. In Revelation 2:13 the apostle John mentions at least one instance of martyrdom during the time he was in exile.

Christ followers were losing their lives.

From A.D. 98 to 117, the emperor Trajan improved the treatment and protections for Christians. His successor, Emperor Hadrian, continued the more favorable treatment. Between A.D. 125 and 160, Christians were, let's say, *tolerated.* Very few Christians were martyred during those decades.

But that all changed in A.D. 161 when Marcus Aurelius became the Roman emperor. Christians suddenly became unpopular. They were blamed for natural disasters because they refused to worship the deities that supposedly protected cities and towns from these natural disasters. Christians were seized, put on trial, and summarily executed.

One example of the kind of persecution under Marcus Aurelius was the arrest of Polycarp, who was the bishop of Smyrna. Smyrna was a coastal city located in western Asia Minor (modern-day Turkey). Smyrna was also the home of one of the seven churches that received a letter from the Lord Jesus through the pen of the apostle John, recorded in the book of Revelation.

Polycarp was arrested and brought before a Roman proconsul. The proconsul encouraged Polycarp to recant his Christian faith:

> "Swear," urged the Proconsul, "reproach Christ, and I will set you free."
>
> "86 years have I have served him," Polycarp declared, "and he has done me no wrong. How can I blaspheme my King and my Savior?"[8]

Polycarp was condemned to death and burned alive. Christ followers were losing their lives.

For the next 150 years, the persecution of Christians ebbed and flowed. Between A.D. 249 and 251, Emperor Decius ordered the persecution of Christians throughout the entire empire. The next emperor, Valerian, tolerated the Christians at first. That didn't last, however. He ordered the deportation of Cyprian, the bishop of Carthage, and Dionysius, the bishop of Alexandria. He closed places of worship and threatened execution of anyone who gathered in these places of worship.

In A.D. 258, Cyprian was summoned from his exile location and brought before the governor, Galerius Maximus. Cyprian was ordered to perform a sacrifice to the Roman gods. He refused. The charges brought against him by the proconsul read:

> You have lived a sacrilegious life, and you have gathered around yourself many vicious men in a conspiracy. You have set yourself up as an enemy of the Roman gods and of their sacred rites. And the pious and most religious emperors Valerian and Gallienus

> Augusti, and Valerian, the most noble Caesar, have been unable to bring you back to the observance of their own sacred rituals. Therefore, having been apprehended as the instigator and ringleader of a criminal conspiracy . . . you will be executed.[9]

Conspiracy, illegal association, enmity toward the gods of Rome—these charges formed the basis for the persecutions during the first three centuries.

After Emperor Valerian died, there was relative peace for the Christians living in the Roman Empire for the next 40 years. Following this peace, there was one final wave of persecution that lasted for nearly a decade. It was known as the Great Persecution, and it began under the rule of Emperors Diocletian (in the east) and Maximian (in the west). Churches were destroyed. Christian worship services were outlawed. Bibles were confiscated and burned. Christians who were leaders in society lost their civil rights. Christian citizens lost their freedoms. Christian clergy were required to make sacrifices to the Roman gods or be sent to prison. A year later, all Christians, not just clergy, were required to sacrifice to the gods or face death. Christ followers were losing their lives.

The tide began to turn for Christians when Constantius became the western emperor of Rome. He implemented a policy of tolerance for Christians that was continued by his son Constantine. As Constantine began to accumulate power in the Roman Empire, he endorsed a document known as the Edict of Milan in A.D. 313, which formerly ended the persecution of Christians. Eleven years later, when Constantine defeated his eastern counterpart and became the sole ruler of the entire Roman Empire, he made Christianity the official religion of the empire.

Despite three centuries of periodic persecution, Christianity flourished. What started out as a troupe of thousands became a movement of millions. Despite all the Christians martyred (some historians estimate as many as two million martyred in the first three centuries), Christianity grew exponentially. What began as a perceived cancer on the culture became its spiritual cure.

The growth of Christianity in the first three centuries has been attributed to numerous factors. These factors were all counter to the culture. Here are some of them:

- The teaching of Christ's resurrection produced hope and confidence.
- The gospel's message of forgiveness gave meaning to people's lives.
- The Christian message transformed lives, a transformation that could be seen by others.
- The Christian message spanned racial, ethnic, and cultural barriers.
- The Christian message elevated the status of women from second-class citizens to first-class citizens on par with men.

- Christians served the needs of the sick and poor, even during deadly plagues.
- Christians cared for discarded babies who were exposed to the elements and left to die.

Here's a key takeaway: The growth of the New Testament church didn't occur because Christ followers embraced their culture. Rather, the church grew because it was counter to the culture. And here's another takeaway: Living counter to one's culture is another way of defining what it means to live in exile while living in the world.

It means living our lives torn.

## GOD'S TRUTH FOR MY LIFE

Persecution of Christians still exists today around the world. Open Doors International has identified 50 countries where there is very high or extremely high persecution of Christians. These countries are primarily either on the African or Asian continents, impacting the lives of an estimated 365 million Christians.[10]

Which of the following cultural categories contribute to the persecution of Christians around the world today? Give an example where applicable.

- Government
- Business
- Education

- Religion
- Media
- Science and Technology
- Arts and Entertainment
- Social Norms

Of the seven factors that led to the growth of Christianity in the first three centuries, which ones are key to influencing our current culture? Explain your reasons.

We live as exiles in our culture. We live counter to our culture. We live lives torn, just like Abraham, Isaac, Jacob, Jacob's sons, Moses, God's people exiled to Babylon, Daniel, Esther, and the early Christians.

When it comes to pointing people to what matters most: Jesus . . .

- Describe how your *faith* overrules the *fear* generated by our culture.

- Describe how your *hope* overcomes the *despair* around us.

- Describe how your *love* for God and people overpowers the *hate* that is prevalent in our culture.

# CHAPTER 10

# PETER AND JUDE

So how does the Roman culture of the early Christians during the first centuries after Jesus' ascension compare with our 21st-century culture? Are there any similarities? Are there any differences? Is there anything new under the sun? Can we learn anything from those early Christ followers in how they navigated a culture filled with challenges and opportunities?

Through the New Testament letters of 1 Peter, 2 Peter, and Jude, we'll identify three adversaries that those early Christians faced as they attempted to navigate their culture. We'll also hear Peter and Jude offer words of encouragement, hope, joy, and a clarion call to fight for the faith. And we'll do it from the perspective of what we can learn from those early Christians so we can navigate the culture of the 21st century.

Let's first begin by summarizing the main message of each of these three letters:

- First Peter is a powerful letter of encouragement to persecuted Christians scattered around the known world. Peter urged them to hold on to the truth and live as followers of Jesus.

- Second Peter is a letter reminding Christians about the truth of Jesus and the need to grow in their faith. He warned about false teachers who would infiltrate the church and teach destructive heresies.
- Jude is a letter encouraging Christians to **"contend for the faith that was once for all entrusted to God's holy people"** (1:3) and to watch out for people **"who pervert the grace of our God into a license for immorality and deny Jesus Christ"** (1:4).

## THREE ADVERSARIES

According to 1 Peter, the early Christ followers faced three adversaries to their faith. We face them too. One of the three was from within. The other two were from the outside, threats from the culture. They are threats to all Christians, whether living in the 1st century or today in the 21st century.

The adversary within us is *sin*, that three-letter word that encompasses everything we do wrong in our lives along with everything we fail to do right. It's a word that literally means "to miss the mark" of what our holy God expects of us.

The two adversaries outside of us are *suffering as a result of persecution* (depending upon our attitude toward it—more on that later) and *false teachers.* These two adversaries exist within our culture and attack our bodies, minds, and hearts. All three have the potential to disrupt our lives as we strive to navigate the culture as followers of Christ.

Three times in his first letter, Peter encouraged his readers to "be alert and of sober mind":

- **"Therefore, with minds that are alert and fully sober . . ."** (1:13).
- **"The end of all things is near. Therefore be alert and of sober mind so that you may pray"** (4:7).
- **"Be alert and of sober mind. Your enemy the devil prowls around like a roaring lion looking for someone to devour. Resist him, standing firm in the faith"** (5:8,9).

Peter used a pair of words to encourage his readers. The first word, translated as "alert," means "to have sound judgment and to be sensible." The second word, translated as "sober mind," literally means "not to be drunk." Figuratively, it means to be in control of one's thought processes and to be aware of what's going on so one can avoid irrational or misguided thinking. As Christians, we need to be alert to these three adversaries that have the potential to undermine how we navigate a culture that is often hostile to Christians.

## *ADVERSARY #1—SIN*

In his first letter, the apostle Peter was not shy about addressing the Christian's battle with sin. Sin has the potential to destroy our relationship with the God who saved us and to prevent us from successfully navigating the culture in which we live. Five times Peter addressed the need for Christ followers to avoid sin.

1. **"Therefore, rid yourselves of all malice and all deceit, hypocrisy, envy, and slander of every kind"** (1 Peter 2:1).

The apostle was speaking to people who were already followers of Jesus, people who believed in their hearts that Jesus was their Savior and who confessed with their mouths that Jesus was their Lord. These were people who had been saved for all eternity by the life, death, and resurrection of Jesus. The theological word for this is *justification.* In his letter to the Christians living in Rome, the apostle Paul wrote that we **"are justified freely by his grace through the redemption that came by Christ Jesus"** (Romans 3:24).

But the fact that the apostle Peter had to give this encouragement is a reminder to us that living as followers of Jesus this side of heaven is a work in progress. The theological word for this process is *sanctification.* With the power of the Holy Spirit, we strive daily to live sanctified, or holy, lives. In the opening verses of his first letter, the apostle Peter wrote, **"To God's elect, exiles scattered throughout the provinces of Pontus, Galatia, Cappadocia, Asia and Bithynia, who have been chosen according to the foreknowledge of God the Father, through the sanctifying work of the Spirit, to be obedient to Jesus Christ and sprinkled with his blood"** (1:1,2).

To rid ourselves of something means to stop or cease from doing it. And what did the apostle encourage his readers to stop doing in 1 Peter 2:1?

- Malice—Malice is that poisonous feeling of hostility and strong dislike for others. It's a feeling that delights in other people's suffering and misfortune.
- Deceit—Deceit is when a person uses trickery or lies to get their own way or to avoid responsibility for their own actions.
- Hypocrisy—Hypocrisy occurs when a person gives the impression of having a certain motivation or purpose but in reality is pretending or giving a false pretense.
- Envy—Envy is a state of jealousy, a feeling of ill will toward other people because of their lives, possessions, or accomplishments.
- Slander—Slander occurs when a person speaks against or speaks evil of another person. It occurs when a person belittles another or runs them down.

Each of these originates in the heart and spills over into words and actions. All of them were as common in the first-century culture as they are today. They were the norm for how people in the first-century culture acted. The apostle Peter, without actually saying the words, encouraged his fellow Christ followers not to reflect the culture but to be counterculture.

2. **"Dear friends, I urge you, as foreigners and exiles, to abstain from sinful desires, which wage war against your soul"** (1 Peter 2:11).

Wow! There is so much that the apostle Peter packed into this one sentence!

The apostle addressed his readers as his "friends." But the word means so much more than that. The word that occurs in the original Greek is derived from the word *love*. Peter loved the people to whom he was writing, and he wanted them to know that.

The apostle also reminded his readers of their current status in the world—"foreigners and exiles." Peter used two different Greek words that mean essentially the same thing. As we noted in chapter 1 of this book with the example of the snowbirds, a foreigner or an exile is a person who for a period of time lives in a place that is not his or her normal residence, a temporary resident.

Here Peter wasn't contrasting countries of the world, states of a nation, or where one's citizenship resides. He was contrasting our temporary residency here on this earth with our permanent residency in heaven. The apostle wanted his readers to remember that they were just passing through this world. We are too. We're temporary residents of this third rock from the sun. Recall what the hymn writer penned in the early 1800s: "I'm but a stranger here. Heaven is my home."

With that reminder, the apostle urged his dear, loved

friends "to abstain from sinful desires." The verb tense that Peter used indicated that this wasn't a one-time action. It was continuous. We could translate it as "to keep abstaining" or "to continue abstaining." Abstinence from sinful desires is an ongoing effort.

Sinful desires are those desires and resulting activities that are morally wrong according to what God has said in his Word. Jesus put it this way: **"For out of the heart come evil thoughts—murder, adultery, sexual immorality, theft, false testimony, slander"** (Matthew 15:19). Sinful actions are the result of sinful desires that spring up in our hearts.

Why do we need to abstain from sinful desires? As Peter indicated, "They wage war against [our souls]." We are in a war, not just a culture war but one that is being waged in our hearts and minds. Sinful desires are a threat to our spiritual lives. These desires have the potential to take over and destroy the Christian faith within us. These sinful desires also have the potential to derail our attempts to navigate our culture successfully as followers of Christ.

3. **"Live as free people, but do not use your freedom as a cover-up for evil"** (1 Peter 2:16).

In Galatians chapter 5, the apostle Paul wrote about the Christian freedom we have because of what Jesus did for us:

> **You, my brothers and sisters, were called to be free. But do not use your freedom to indulge the**

> **flesh; rather, serve one another humbly in love. For the entire law is fulfilled in keeping this one command: "Love your neighbor as yourself." If you bite and devour each other, watch out or you will be destroyed by each other.**
>
> **So I say, walk by the Spirit, and you will not gratify the desires of the flesh.** (verses 13–16)

In his first letter, the apostle Peter said much the same thing. He reminded his readers that as followers of Christ, we live in freedom. We have been set free from having to keep the law in order to win God's favor. Keep in mind that sin has made the law both a curse and a burden. We have also been set free to live for the glory of God. Our freedom is not to be used to cover up or excuse sin. That would make a mockery of God's grace. The apostle Peter urged his fellow Christians not to cover up evil with the gift of grace and the freedom they'd been given.

4. **"Do not repay evil with evil or insult with insult"** (1 Peter 3:9).

The concept of *repayment*, or *recompense*, can be a positive or a negative activity. The words themselves are neutral. Here, the "evil" and the "insult" reveal that this is a negative thing to be avoided. So what does this look like?

The scenario that the apostle laid out involved another

person initiating some kind of evil or insult. Peter encouraged his readers not to get into a potentially nasty payback cycle with the other person.

The word *evil* pertains to anything that is bad, harmful, or damaging. The evil could consist of harsh words, quarrels, fighting words, coldhearted actions, controlling activities, and the desire for revenge, just to name a few.

To insult someone is to say mean things to the person or about the person. It can include name-calling and slander. Peter encouraged his readers not to take any action if someone hurled insults at them. Don't insult them back. It can lead to some pretty unspiritual scenarios.

5. **"Therefore, since Christ suffered in his body, arm yourselves also with the same attitude, because whoever suffers in the body is done with sin. As a result, they do not live the rest of their earthly lives for evil human desires, but rather for the will of God. For you have spent enough time in the past doing what pagans choose to do—living in debauchery, lust, drunkenness, orgies, carousing and detestable idolatry. They are surprised that you do not join them in their reckless, wild living, and they heap abuse on you"** (1 Peter 4:1–4).

We'll speak more about suffering and the potential negative impact it can have on followers of Jesus in the next section.

In these verses, the apostle Peter encouraged his readers to make their spiritual lives a priority over their physical lives and human desires. Peter pointed out that when a person becomes a Christ follower, priorities change, attitudes change, and activities change. No longer do they live the rest of their lives on this earth pursuing sinful human desires. Instead, they pursue lives in alignment with the will of God.

Peter listed six sinful human desires and activities that were common in first-century culture, all to be avoided:

- Debauchery—behavior that was morally unrestrained; extreme immorality with the implication of sexual decadence.
- Lust—a strong desire to have what belongs to someone else or to engage in an activity that is morally wrong.
- Drunkenness—intoxication that refers to consumption of a large quantity of wine.
- Orgies—drinking parties where the participants engaged in the consumption of alcoholic beverages leading to unrestrained immoral sexual behavior.
- Carousing—drinking matches or bouts where large quantities of alcoholic beverages were consumed.
- Detestable idolatry—disgusting practices involved in idol worship, typically sexual in nature.

Even though a first-century Christian didn't want to engage in any of these, they were a temptation to Peter's audience and always will be as long as we're this side of heaven. Peter also acknowledged that for some in his audience, these sinful activities were a part of their pre-Christian lives.

These six sinful activities are a threat to every Christ follower today as well. Any one of them can lead us away from the Jesus we love and serve. Each one has the potential to sidetrack our desire to navigate the culture in which we live as followers of Christ.

By not engaging in these activities, Peter pointed out a potential result: **"They are surprised that you do not join them in their reckless, wild living, and they heap abuse on you"** (1 Peter 4:4). Those in the culture who reflected the cultural norms were surprised that the followers of Christ didn't engage in those cultural norms. It was a testimony to the fact that those early Christ followers were living countercultural lives.

Five times in his first letter, the apostle Peter addressed the need for Christians to avoid sin. Sin is an enemy to our faith, and it can prevent us from being true to the God who made us and saved us.

## *ADVERSARY #2—SUFFERING*

In his first letter, the apostle Peter addressed the topic of suffering. Seventeen times the word *suffer* occurs in this letter. As we alluded to at the beginning of this chapter, suffering *can be* an enemy of the Christian, depending on one's attitude toward it.

It's human nature to think of suffering as undesirable and unwelcome. No one ever seems to say, "I enjoy suffering." Suffering can occur because of bad personal choices or because of the choices of others, whether intentional or unintentional. Suffering can occur as the result of health issues or accidents or war or weather or a dozen other causes. Suffering can also show up in the form of persecution as the result of what is happening in our society and culture. There are many different sources of suffering.

The reactions and responses to suffering vary widely. Some of the most common human responses to suffering are bitterness, resentment, and anger. These negative emotions are sometimes directed at other people, but often they're directed at God. Why would a loving God allow me to suffer? This is an often-asked question by those who are blaming God for their situation. This response to suffering can be a serious threat to Christ followers because it calls into question God's love for them.

The Christians to whom the apostle wrote this letter were experiencing suffering, primarily caused by persecution. But Peter didn't approach suffering through the lens of bitterness, anger, or playing the blame game. Instead, he approached suffering from how God uses suffering to accomplish his will.

Let's see what Peter had to say about suffering at the beginning of his letter, immediately following his opening greeting:

**Praise be to the God and Father of our Lord Jesus Christ! In his great mercy he has given us new birth into a living hope through the resurrection of Jesus Christ from the dead, and into an inheritance that can never perish, spoil or fade. This inheritance is kept in heaven for you, who through faith are shielded by God's power until the coming of the salvation that is ready to be revealed in the last time. In all this you greatly rejoice, though now for a little while you may have had to suffer grief in all kinds of trials. These have come so that the proven genuineness of your faith—of greater worth than gold, which perishes even though refined by fire—may result in praise, glory and honor when Jesus Christ is revealed.** (1 Peter 1:3-7)

Peter put the suffering that those early Christians were experiencing into a context that had eternal implications. The people to whom Peter was writing had received a new birth, new hope, and a new inheritance through the resurrection of Jesus. Because of Jesus' resurrection, they possessed eternal life, guaranteed by the resurrection of Jesus. It was a reason for them to rejoice even though they suffered temporary grief in all kinds of trials. Their momentary trials paled by comparison with their eternal inheritance. Even if their suffering would end in physical death, they would still have life, eternal life in heaven.

Peter then went on to explain a specific reason why

these followers of Christ were suffering trials. Their suffering proved the genuineness of their faith, which the author compared to gold ore. Gold ore is refined through the smelting process to become pure and useful. Faith, which is far more valuable than gold, is purified and strengthened through suffering. Suffering has a way of refocusing our attention on the words and promises of our God.

Several verses later, Peter captured this same thought by focusing on the sufferings of Jesus and the result that came from his suffering: **"the sufferings of the Messiah and the glories that would follow"** (1 Peter 1:11). Because of what Jesus did for us, we get to enjoy the glory of heaven with him.

In chapter 2 of this letter, Peter gave a practical example of suffering when he addressed those in servitude to others. When you see the word *slave* in the New Testament, don't think of the ugly racial slavery that plagued the U.S. prior to the Civil War. Instead, think of a person in servitude as a household servant, a farmhand, or even an employee.

In the first-century Roman world, people found themselves in servitude either because they were captives of war or because they made poor economic choices and had to pay off their debts. Unlike the slavery of later centuries, Roman slaves were always entitled to food, clothing, and lodging. They could own property, get married, and had the ability to buy their freedom. For many in servitude, it was actually economically advantageous. With this practical example, the apostle also framed it in a spiritual and eternal context:

**Slaves, in reverent fear of God submit yourselves to your masters, not only to those who are good and considerate, but also to those who are harsh. For it is commendable if someone bears up under the pain of unjust suffering because they are conscious of God. But how is it to your credit if you receive a beating for doing wrong and endure it? But if you suffer for doing good and you endure it, this is commendable before God. To this you were called, because Christ suffered for you, leaving you an example, that you should follow in his steps.**

**"He committed no sin, and no deceit was found in his mouth."**

**When they hurled their insults at him, he did not retaliate; when he suffered, he made no threats. Instead, he entrusted himself to him who judges justly. "He himself bore our sins" in his body on the cross, so that we might die to sins and live for righteousness; "by his wounds you have been healed." For "you were like sheep going astray," but now you have returned to the Shepherd and Overseer of your souls.** (1 Peter 2:18–25)

Peter recognized that followers of Christ may experience suffering at the hands of a harsh master or boss. He also differentiated between suffering that is deserved and that which is not. If a Christ follower suffers for doing good, this is something that is commendable before God.

The apostle then framed this in a spiritual and eternal context. Peter referred to Christ as the Christian's example. Even though Jesus was sinless, he suffered. When sinful human beings targeted Jesus for suffering, he didn't retaliate or make threats. Instead, he entrusted himself to his heavenly Father and went the way of the cross so that by his wounds we might be healed of our sins and empowered to live holy lives.

There is a Latin saying that helps us better understand Peter's letters: *repetitio est mater studiorum.* It means "repetition is the mother of learning." Peter used repetition repeatedly in this letter, especially when he was addressing the subject of suffering. In chapter 3, the apostle Peter repeated the same thought that we just considered in chapter 2:

> **For it is better, if it is God's will, to suffer for doing good than for doing evil. For Christ also suffered once for sins, the righteous for the unrighteous, to bring you to God. He was put to death in the body but made alive in the Spirit. After being made alive, he went and made proclamation to the imprisoned spirits—to those who were disobedient long ago when God waited patiently in the days of Noah while the ark was being built. In it only a few people, eight in all, were saved through water,**

> **and this water symbolizes baptism that now saves you also—not the removal of dirt from the body but the pledge of a clear conscience toward God. It saves you by the resurrection of Jesus Christ, who has gone into heaven and is at God's right hand—with angels, authorities and powers in submission to him.** (1 Peter 3:17-22)

Peter addressed the suffering of the early Christians and again related it back to the suffering of Christ and the spiritual/eternal blessings that flowed from his suffering.

In chapter 4, Peter made a statement about suffering that needs some unpacking and clarification. He wrote, **"Therefore, since Christ suffered in his body, arm yourselves also with the same attitude, because whoever suffers in the body is done with sin"** (1 Peter 4:1). To do the unpacking and clarifying, let's tap the insights of the original speaker for Time of Grace Ministry, Pastor Mark Jeske. Pastor Jeske wrote a commentary on 1 Peter (also the letters of 2 Peter, James, and Jude). This is how he explained this short but challenging verse:

> The first and greatest meaning of the sufferings of Christ is that in this way he made substitutionary payment for the sins of the world. But there is a second meaning, and Peter describes it in this section on our response to the mighty objective truths of the gospel described in 3:18-22.

> The second implication is that just as Christ sacrificed his body for us, we need to be ready to sacrifice earthly gain and physical desires in order to place spiritual priorities first. That's what Peter means when he says, "He who has suffered in his body is done with sin." That doesn't mean that our personal suffering brings forgiveness of sin. It does mean that persecution and suffering can have the beneficial effect of stripping away sinful distractions from our lives and lifting our focus higher. Suffering can be a harsh but effective cure for materialism. One has a lot more time for prayer in a jail cell, isn't it so? Peter's point is to help his suffering friends see that their persecutions are not the ultimate disaster or proof that God no longer cares for them. The reverse is true—God is using these hardships to refine and purify their desires and priorities more closely to reflect his will.[11]

This is another example of *repetitio est mater studiorum* in Peter's letter. Repetition reinforced Peter's point to his readers. And he repeated his point *again* in 1 Peter 4:12–19:

> **Dear friends, do not be surprised at the fiery ordeal that has come on you to test you, as though something strange were happening to you. But rejoice inasmuch as you participate in the sufferings of Christ, so that you may be overjoyed**

**when his glory is revealed. If you are insulted because of the name of Christ, you are blessed, for the Spirit of glory and of God rests on you. If you suffer, it should not be as a murderer or thief or any other kind of criminal, or even as a meddler. However, if you suffer as a Christian, do not be ashamed, but praise God that you bear that name. For it is time for judgment to begin with God's household; and if it begins with us, what will the outcome be for those who do not obey the gospel of God? And,**

**"If it is hard for the righteous to be saved, what will become of the ungodly and the sinner?"**

**So then, those who suffer according to God's will should commit themselves to their faithful Creator and continue to do good.**

From this section of Peter's letter, we have five takeaways:

- We shouldn't be surprised that we have to endure suffering because of our relationship with Jesus.
- We rejoice that we are able to participate in the sufferings of Christ (because the temporary pain pales in comparison to the eternal joy that will be ours).

- We are blessed if we are insulted because of Jesus.
- We aren't ashamed of having to suffer as a Christian. Rather, we praise God.
- When we suffer for doing God's will, we recommit ourselves to him and continue to do good.

Finally, in chapter 5 as he concluded his first letter (did you notice that Peter addressed suffering in *every* part of his letter), he focused on the matter of suffering one last time:

> **Humble yourselves, therefore, under God's mighty hand, that he may lift you up in due time. Cast all your anxiety on him because he cares for you.**
>
> **Be alert and of sober mind. Your enemy the devil prowls around like a roaring lion looking for someone to devour. Resist him, standing firm in the faith, because you know that the family of believers throughout the world is undergoing the same kind of sufferings.**
>
> **And the God of all grace, who called you to his eternal glory in Christ, after you have suffered a little while, will himself restore you and make you strong, firm and steadfast. To him be the power for ever and ever. Amen.** (verses 6–11)

Peter concluded his letter by pointing out the real enemy behind the potential enemy of suffering—the devil. This familiar verse of the devil prowling around like a roaring lion occurred within the context of suffering. The context is significant. When a Christ follower faces suffering, he or she becomes more vulnerable to the attacks of the devil. So Peter encouraged those early Christians to be awake and alert! Resist him! Stand firm in the faith!

And let's not miss Peter's final encouragements. Cast all your anxiety on Christ! He cares for you! After you have suffered a little while, he'll restore you! He'll make you strong, firm, and steadfast!

Say it with me, "Amen!"

## *ADVERSARY #3—FALSE TEACHERS*

Unlike suffering, which *can be* an adversary of Christians depending on our attitude toward it, false teachers definitely are. Both the apostle Peter in his second letter and Jude in his letter tackle the issue of false teachers in the New Testament church.

What's most interesting about these two letters, when it comes to addressing false teachers, is that they say essentially the same thing, often using similar words and phrases. It appears that either Peter or Jude borrowed content from the other. That isn't unusual in the biblical text. Old Testament authors borrowed or quoted content from authors who lived before them. Jesus himself quoted the Old Testament many times. New Testament authors also quoted the Old

Testament on many occasions. So it isn't out of the ordinary that Peter quoted Jude or Jude quoted Peter.

So who was the original author, and who borrowed the content for their letter? It's impossible to determine the answer to that question. It seems to me though, that the more fiery style of writing in 2 Peter chapter 2 is a bit different from the style of Peter's first letter and the other chapters of his second letter. That would suggest to me that Peter addressed the issue of false teachers using some of the content of Jude's letter. But we don't know that for sure.

Let's look at a side-by-side comparison of 2 Peter chapter 2 and Jude 1:3-19 that addressed the false teachers who had infiltrated the early church. What Peter and Jude especially describe is the inward motivation of false teachers and the judgment of God that will come upon them.

As you read through this side-by-side comparison, underline or highlight the characteristics and the motivation of these false teachers as well as the statements of God's judgment on them.

| 2 Peter 2:1–22; 3:3 (GW) | Jude 1:3–19 (GW) |
|---|---|
| | [3] Dear friends, I had intended to write to you about the salvation we share. But something has come up. It demands that I write to you and encourage you to continue your fight for the Christian faith that was entrusted to God's holy people once for all time. |
| [1] False prophets were among God's people in the past, as false teachers will be among you. They will secretly bring in their own destructive teachings. They will deny the Lord, who has bought them, and they will bring themselves swift destruction. | [4] Some people have slipped in among you unnoticed. Not long ago they were condemned in writing for the following reason: They are people to whom God means nothing. They use God's kindness as an excuse for sexual freedom and deny our only Master and Lord, Jesus Christ. |
| [2] Many people will follow them in their sexual freedom and will cause others to dishonor the way of truth. [3] In their greed they will use good-sounding arguments to exploit you. The verdict . . . | |

| 2 Peter 2:1–22; 3:3 (GW) | Jude 1:3–19 (GW) |
|---|---|
| . . . against them from long ago is still in force, and their destruction is not asleep. | |
| | [5] I want to remind you about what you already know: The Lord once saved his people from Egypt. But on another occasion he destroyed those who didn't believe. |
| [4] God didn't spare angels who sinned. He threw them into hell, where he has secured them with chains of darkness and is holding them for judgment. | [6] He held angels for judgment on the great day. They were held in darkness, bound by eternal chains. These are the angels who didn't keep their position of authority but abandoned their assigned place. |
| [5] God didn't spare the ancient world either. He brought the flood on the world of ungodly people, but he protected Noah and seven other people. Noah was his messenger who told people about the kind of life that has God's approval. | |

| 2 Peter 2:1–22; 3:3 (GW) | Jude 1:3–19 (GW) |
| --- | --- |
| [6] God condemned the cities of Sodom and Gomorrah and destroyed them by burning them to ashes. He made those cities an example to ungodly people of what is going to happen to them. | [7] What happened to Sodom and Gomorrah and the cities near them is an example for us of the punishment of eternal fire. The people of these cities suffered the same fate that God's people and the angels did, because they committed sexual sins and engaged in homosexual activities. |
| [7] Yet, God rescued Lot, a man who had his approval. Lot was distressed by the lifestyle of people who had no principles and lived in sexual freedom. [8] Although he was a man who had God's approval, he lived among the people of Sodom and Gomorrah. Each day was like torture to him as he saw and heard the immoral things that people did. | |
| [9] Since the Lord did all this, he knows how to rescue godly people when they are tested. He also knows how to hold immoral people for punishment on the day of judgment. | |

| 2 Peter 2:1–22; 3:3 (GW) | Jude 1:3–19 (GW) |
|---|---|
| [10] This is especially true of those who follow their corrupt nature along the path of impure desires and who despise the Lord's authority. | [8] Yet, in a similar way, the people who slipped in among you are dreamers. They contaminate their bodies with sin, reject the Lord's authority, and insult his glory. |
| | [9] When the archangel Michael argued with the devil, they were arguing over the body of Moses. But Michael didn't dare to hand down a judgment against the devil. Instead, Michael said, "May the Lord reprimand you!" |
| These false teachers are bold and arrogant. They aren't afraid to insult the Lord's glory. [11] Angels, who have more strength and power than these teachers, don't bring an insulting judgment against them from the Lord. [12] These false teachers insult what they don't understand. | [10] Whatever these people don't understand, they insult. |

| 2 Peter 2:1–22; 3:3 (GW) | Jude 1:3–19 (GW) |
| --- | --- |
| They are like animals, which are creatures of instinct that are born to be caught and killed. So they will be destroyed like animals. | Like animals, which are creatures of instinct, they use whatever they know to destroy themselves. |
| (See verses 15,16.) | [11] How horrible it will be for them! They have followed the path of Cain. They have rushed into Balaam's error to make a profit. They have rebelled like Korah and destroyed themselves. |
| [13] These false teachers are stains and blemishes. They take pleasure in holding wild parties in broad daylight. | |
| They especially enjoy deceiving you while they eat with you. | [12] These people are a disgrace at the special meals you share with other believers. They eat with you and don't feel ashamed. They are shepherds who care only for themselves. |

| 2 Peter 2:1–22; 3:3 (GW) | Jude 1:3–19 (GW) |
|---|---|
| [14] They're always looking for an adulterous woman. They can't stop looking for sin as they seduce people who aren't sure of what they believe. Their minds are focused on their greed. They are cursed. | (See verse 11.) |
| [15] These false teachers have left the straight path and wandered off to follow the path of Balaam, son of Beor. Balaam loved what his wrongdoing earned him. [16] But he was convicted for his evil. A donkey, which normally can't talk, spoke with a human voice and wouldn't allow the prophet to continue his insanity. | |
| [17] These false teachers are dried-up springs. They are a mist blown around by a storm. Gloomy darkness has been kept for them. | They are dry clouds blown around by the winds. They are withered, uprooted trees without any fruit. As a result, they have died twice. [13] Their shame is like the foam on the wild waves of the sea. They are wandering stars for whom gloomy darkness is kept forever. |

| 2 Peter 2:1–22; 3:3 (GW) | Jude 1:3–19 (GW) |
|---|---|
| | [14] Furthermore, Enoch, from the seventh generation after Adam, prophesied about them. He said, "The Lord has come with countless thousands of his holy angels. [15] He has come to judge all these people. He has come to convict all these ungodly sinners for all the ungodly things they have done and all the harsh things they have said about him." |
| [18] They arrogantly use nonsense to seduce people by appealing to their sexual desires, especially to sexual freedom. They seduce people who have just escaped from those who live in error. | [16] These people complain, find fault, follow their own desires, say arrogant things, and flatter people in order to take advantage of them. |
| [19] They promise these people freedom, but they themselves are slaves to corruption. A person is a slave to whatever he gives in to. | |

| 2 Peter 2:1–22; 3:3 (GW) | Jude 1:3–19 (GW) |
|---|---|
| [20] People can know our Lord and Savior Jesus Christ and escape the world's filth. But if they get involved in this filth again and give in to it, they are worse off than they were before. [21] It would have been better for them never to have known the way of life that God approves of than to know it and turn their backs on the holy life God told them to live. [22] These proverbs have come true for them: "A dog goes back to its vomit," and "A sow that has been washed goes back to roll around in the mud." | |
| [3:3] First, you must understand this: In the last days people who follow their own desires will appear. | [17] Dear friends, remember what the apostles of our Lord Jesus Christ told you to expect: [18] "In the last times people who ridicule God will appear. They will follow their own ungodly desires." [19] These are the people who cause divisions. They are concerned about physical things, not spiritual things. |

What are the key takeaways from what Peter and Jude wrote? Let's again tap into the biblical insights of Pastor Mark Jeske who, in his commentary on 2 Peter, identified seven key points about false teachers:

So, what points does Peter make?

1. *False teachers will certainly come.* Satan will try to wreck the church not only by assault from the outside, by persecution and government opposition, but by rotting out the church from within. False teachers often use comfortable, traditional terminology; they do not generally advertise that they are subverting the Bible. By working within the church structure, they can gain a large following. It is never safe to determine the truth based on the number of adherents to a particular idea.
2. *False teachers have certain characteristics.* Peter mentions a few in general terms:
    - They deny the sovereign Lord who bought them.
    - They pass off their own thoughts as the Word of God.
    - They despise and reject authority.
    - They promise freedom, but this results only in slavery.
    - They blaspheme the "glories."
    - They hide a foul and corrupt personal life—adultery, greed, materialism.

3. *False teachers are hurting other people.* They are making the way of truth look bad. They are dragging recently saved people back into unbelief. Their heresies are not harmless differences of opinion, but they destroy. People are seduced away from Christ by them.

4. *False teachers are rotten inside.* The Spirit of the Lord who spoke through Peter could see into these people's hearts and reveal what was in there. We cannot read the minds and hearts of others, but God can. Peter says that false teachers are motivated not by an earnest desire for the truth but rather by greed, corrupt desires, and love of money and pleasure.

5. *God knows the truth about false teachers.* Peter tells God's opinion of them: they are not true prophets but false; they despise authority; they are bold, arrogant, greedy, pleasure-loving, brute beasts, an accursed brood, empty, boastful, depraved, and blasphemous.

6. *God's judgment and punishment are certain.* It may seem as if false teachers are getting away with lying in God's name and succeeding. Not so. God says that their destruction is certain and will be swift and sudden. God will take care of business, as he did with the evil and rebellious angels, with the people at the time of the flood, and with Sodom and Gomorrah. There will be justice in the end. False teachers will perish like beasts, in utter darkness.

7. *God will rescue the faithful.* God will rescue believers

> from this peril even as he rescued Noah from destruction by water and Lot from destruction by fire.[12]

What Peter and Jude wrote about false teachers was quite general in nature. Neither one identified any false teachers by name or location. We know from other letters in the New Testament of two specific groups of false teachers. Whether they're the same ones Peter and Jude had in mind, we just don't know.

When the apostle Paul wrote his letter to the Galatians, he mentioned a group known as the Judaizers. The word *Judaizer* comes from a Greek verb meaning "to live according to Jewish customs." The Judaizers claimed that salvation was attained through a combination of God's grace and human effort. Satan used those inside the church to undermine the church.

When the apostle Paul wrote his letter to the Christians living in Colossae, he warned them about the teachings of a group known as the Gnostics (*gnosis* is Greek for "knowledge"). The Gnostics attacked the adequacy and supremacy of Christ (1:15,19; 2:2,9). They claimed that something beyond Jesus was needed to defeat the power of demons (1:6; 2:10,15). They also insisted on observing special days and rituals (2:16,21), revealing themselves as legalists. Another sect of Gnostics claimed that what people did with their bodies didn't matter if their spirits were aligned with God, thus encouraging immorality. There are more examples in the letter to the Colossians, but you get the picture. They may not be called Gnostics any longer, but Satan still uses this tactic to undermine the church from within.

Again, whether Peter and Jude were referring to either the Judaizers or the Gnostics, we just don't know. There certainly could have been other false teachers or other groups of false teachers. Or Peter and Jude may have written a composite of all the false teachers that had infiltrated the early church. No matter who they were or where they lived, they were adversaries of the first-century church and enemies of God.

In the letters of Peter and Jude, we've examined the lives of those early followers of Christ living in exile in the New Testament world. So far we've considered nothing but challenges—persecution and three adversaries: sin, suffering, and false teachers.

How about some good news? How about the opportunities we have?

## THE CHOSEN

In both of Peter's letters, there are several threads that weave through the pages. One thread describes who these first-century Christ followers were from God's perspective. They were *the chosen*. Another thread focuses on the love, hope, and joy that these early believers expressed to God and to one another.

Peter wasted no time addressing the first thread:

**Peter, an apostle of Jesus Christ,**

**to God's *elect*, exiles scattered throughout the provinces of Pontus, Galatia, Cappadocia, Asia and Bithynia, who have been *chosen* according to the foreknowledge of God the Father, through the sanctifying work of the Spirit, to be obedient to Jesus Christ and sprinkled with his blood:**

**Grace and peace be yours in abundance.**
(1 Peter 1:1,2)

Peter reminded the exiles scattered throughout Asia Minor that they were *elect* and *chosen*. Both of these words indicate that these exiles didn't become followers of Christ by chance. Not at all. It was because of God loving them, seeking them, and through the sanctifying work of the Spirit bringing them to faith in Jesus. They were chosen.

In the Old Testament, the Lord God had his chosen people. They were the descendants of Abraham, Isaac, and Jacob. After Jesus walked this earth, died, rose again, and ascended into heaven, God's chosen people were now those who believed in Jesus.

One of the most beautiful sections in the Bible that speaks to us about followers of Christ being chosen is 1 Peter chapter 2. But as we'll see, this section begins with someone else being chosen first, which needed to happened if we were ever to be chosen:

**As you come to him, the living Stone—rejected by**

humans but chosen by God and precious to him—you also, like living stones, are being built into a spiritual house to be a holy priesthood, offering spiritual sacrifices acceptable to God through Jesus Christ. For in Scripture it says:

> "See, I lay a stone in Zion,
> a chosen and precious cornerstone,
> and the one who trusts in him
> will never be put to shame."

Now to you who believe, this stone is precious. But to those who do not believe,

> "The stone the builders rejected
> has become the cornerstone,"

and,

> "A stone that causes people to stumble
> and a rock that makes them fall."

They stumble because they disobey the message—which is also what they were destined for.

But you are a chosen people, a royal priesthood, a holy nation, God's special possession, that you may declare the praises of him who called you out

> **of darkness into his wonderful light. Once you were not a people, but now you are the people of God; once you had not received mercy, but now you have received mercy.** (1 Peter 2:4-10)

Using the analogy of a building, Peter described a living Stone that, although this Stone had been rejected by humans, was chosen by God and precious to him. That Stone was God's eternal Son, who became a human being to carry out God's rescue plan. Peter then went on to describe the Christians to whom he was writing. They too were stones, living stones.

The analogy continued. Both the Stone and the living stones were built into a spiritual house with Christ as the cornerstone and all his followers being the stones of the house. This analogy is of the church. As members of the church, those early Christ followers were able—because of Jesus' life, death, and resurrection—to approach God in worship and prayer as members of a holy priesthood. No longer did God's chosen people have to go through a high priest to have access to God, as it was in the Old Testament. No, because of Jesus they had direct access to God. And we do too!

It's worth mentioning that Peter cited three Old Testament passages that foreshadowed the Stone chosen by God. The first passage was from Isaiah 28:16, the second from Psalm 118:22, and the third from Isaiah 8:14. All three passages spoke about the Stone. The last passage spoke about those who didn't believe that Jesus was the Son of God and this world's Rescuer. Their rejection of Jesus would result in them being rejected by God.

Then Peter wrapped a big bright bow around this beautiful section with words that, in my opinion, every Christian should commit to memory. That's because they are words that remind us just who we are and what we are called to be and do:

- We are a chosen people, chosen by God himself!
- We are a royal priesthood with direct access to God to worship him!
- We are the eternal God's special possession, bought with the blood of Jesus!
- No longer do we live in the darkness of sin and unbelief!
- God has brought us into the light of the Light of world!

What a loving and merciful God we have to do that all for us! No matter what persecution surfaces, no matter how the culture we live in targets us or seeks to undermine our walk with Christ, no matter what life looks like as an exile, no matter how torn we feel, we remain *the chosen*, the people of God!

When Peter wrote his second letter, he again wasted no time addressing the first thread. He reminded his readers of their calling and election in the first and third paragraphs that follow. But tucked in between, Peter addressed the beautiful qualities of God's chosen ones, qualities that could grow and mature and cause them to flourish in their lives. His second letter, after the opening greeting, begins:

> **His divine power has given us everything we need for a godly life through our knowledge of him who called us by his own glory and goodness. Through these he has given us his very great and precious promises, so that through them you may participate in the divine nature, having escaped the corruption in the world caused by evil desires.**
>
> **For this very reason, make every effort to add to your faith *goodness*; and to goodness, *knowledge*; and to knowledge, *self-control*; and to self-control, *perseverance*; and to perseverance, *godliness*; and to godliness, *mutual affection*; and to mutual affection, *love*. For if you possess these qualities in increasing measure, they will keep you from being ineffective and unproductive in your knowledge of our Lord Jesus Christ. But whoever does not have them is nearsighted and blind, forgetting that they have been cleansed from their past sins.**
>
> **Therefore, my brothers and sisters, make every effort to confirm your calling and election. For if you do these things, you will never stumble, and**

> **you will receive a rich welcome into the eternal kingdom of our Lord and Savior Jesus Christ.** (2 Peter 1:3–11)

Then throughout both letters, Peter reminded God's chosen ones of the impact from the blessings of being God's chosen ones. Note the words in italics of love, hope, and joy:

> **Praise be to the God and Father of our Lord Jesus Christ! In his great mercy he has given us new birth into *a living hope* through the resurrection of Jesus Christ from the dead, and into an inheritance that can never perish, spoil or fade. This inheritance is kept in heaven for you, who through faith are shielded by God's power until the coming of the salvation that is ready to be revealed in the last time. In all this *you greatly rejoice*, though now for a little while you may have had to suffer grief in all kinds of trials. These have come so that the proven genuineness of your faith—of greater worth than gold, which perishes even though refined by fire—may result in praise, glory and honor when Jesus Christ is revealed. Though you have not seen him, *you love him*; and even though you do not see him now, you believe in him and are *filled with an inexpressible and glorious joy*, for you are receiving the end result of your faith, the salvation of your souls.** (1 Peter 1:3–9)

Finally, six more times in his first letter, Peter offered encouragement to the chosen ones for how to live their lives for God and for people in their culture. These six encouragements can be our lampposts for how we navigate our contemporary culture throughout our lives. Note again the words in italics:

- **"Through him you believe in God, who raised him from the dead and glorified him, and so your faith and hope are in God. Now that you have purified yourselves by obeying the truth so that you have sincere love for each other, *love one another deeply*, from the heart. For you have been born again, not of perishable seed, but of imperishable, through the living and enduring word of God"** (1 Peter 1:21–23).

- **"Live such *good lives* among the pagans that, though they accuse you of doing wrong, they may see your *good deeds* and glorify God on the day he visits us"** (1 Peter 2:12).

- **"Finally, all of you, be like-minded, *be sympathetic*, *love one another*, *be compassionate and humble*. Do not repay evil with evil or insult with insult. On the contrary, *repay evil with blessing*, because to this you were called so that you may inherit a blessing"** (1 Peter 3:8,9).

- **"But in your hearts *revere Christ as Lord*. Always *be prepared to give an answer* to everyone who asks you to give the reason *for the hope that you have*. But do this with *gentleness and respect*"** (1 Peter 3:15).

- **"The end of all things is near. Therefore be alert and of sober mind so that you may *pray*. Above all, *love each other deeply*, because love covers over a multitude of sins. *Offer hospitality* to one another without grumbling. Each of you should *use whatever gift you have received to serve others*, as faithful stewards of God's grace in its various forms. If anyone speaks, they should do so as one who speaks the very words of God. If anyone serves, they should do so with the strength God provides, *so that in all things God may be praised through Jesus Christ*. To him be the glory and the power for ever and ever. Amen"** (1 Peter 4:7-11).

- **"But *rejoice* inasmuch as you participate in the sufferings of Christ, *so that you may be overjoyed when his glory is revealed*"** (1 Peter 4:13).

Through the New Testament letters of 1 and 2 Peter and Jude, we've identified three adversaries the early Christians faced in their culture. At the same time, Peter reminded his fellow Christians who they were—the chosen ones who enjoyed God's blessings and protections. We also heard Peter offer words of encouragement to live our lives loving Jesus, loving people, and pointing people to what matters most: Jesus!

Of all these encouragements from Peter, which one touches your heart the most? Which one gives you the greatest comfort?

## GOD'S TRUTH FOR MY LIFE

There were two external adversaries that the early Christians faced in their culture. Give two or three examples of how those two adversaries (suffering and false teachers) show up in our own culture.

What are the two or three attitudes, actions, or activities in our culture that trouble you the most as a Christ follower?

For each of Peter's six lamppost encouragements, give an example of how you can put those encouragements into practice:

*Love one another deeply.*

*Live such good lives.*

*Repay evil with blessing.*

*Give an answer for the hope you have.*

*Pray, love, offer hospitality, serve others.*

*Rejoice in suffering.*

We live as exiles in our culture. We live counter to our culture. We live lives torn, just like Abraham, Isaac, Jacob, Jacob's sons, Moses, God's people exiled to Babylon, Daniel, Esther, and the early Christians.

When it comes to the attitudes, actions, or activities that trouble you the most in our culture . . .

- Describe how your *faith* overrules the *fear* generated by our culture.

- Describe how your *hope* overcomes the *despair* around us.

- Describe how your *love* for God and people overpowers the *hate* that is prevalent in our culture.

# CONCLUSION

We live torn lives.

Two thousand years ago, the apostle Paul penned a letter to the Christians living in the Greek city of Philippi. I began this book with these words, and I'll end with them. The apostle explained the torn life he lived:

> **For to me, to live is Christ and to die is gain. If I am to go on living in the body, this will mean fruitful labor for me. Yet what shall I choose? I do not know! I am torn between the two: I desire to depart and be with Christ, which is better by far; but it is more necessary for you that I remain in the body.** (Philippians 1:21–24)

Prisoner Paul was torn between departing this life to be with Christ for all eternity (which is better by far) and remaining in this world to fulfill his calling of pointing people to what matters most: Jesus.

The same is true for us. As our culture continues to crash and burn around us, the desire to depart and be with Christ seems to be the better option. Someday we will depart this life. But we don't get to make that choice. Our God has given each of us our own time of grace to answer his call, to participate in his plans, and to carry out his will. For now, it's more necessary for us to remain in this life to serve our God and the people in our lives, even though it means living life torn.

The reason we live torn lives is that we are living as exiles while living in the world. We are exiles, foreigners, strangers in the world, spiritual snowbirds. As exiles, we face many challenges because we live by a different set of beliefs and norms. However, even as exiles, we have opportunities to influence our culture by our words and actions, by loving people, by helping people, and by living such good lives that others wonder why. The Bible is filled with examples of how to live as exiles in this world.

The reason we are living as exiles while living in the world is because of the fact that although we are living *in* this world, we're not *of* the world. Jesus' prayer on the night he was betrayed reminds us of that: **"My prayer is not that you take them out of the world but that you protect them from the evil one. They are not of the world, even as I am not of it"** (John 17:15,16). We are living *in* our culture, but we are not *of* the culture.

The reason we are in the world but not of the world is that we've been chosen. The apostle Peter made that clear: **"But you are a chosen people, a royal priesthood, a holy nation, God's special possession, that you may declare**

**the praises of him who called you out of darkness into his wonderful light"** (1 Peter 2:9). We've been chosen by the Chosen One to be his special people.

Finally, the reason we have been chosen is because of God's tremendous love for us.

> **See what great love the Father has lavished on us, that we should be called children of God! And that is what we are! The reason the world does not know us is that it did not know him. Dear friends, now we are children of God, and what we will be has not yet been made known. But we know that when Christ appears, we shall be like him, for we shall see him as he is."** (1 John 3:1,2)

When Christ returns, we'll live with him in the new heaven and the new earth where there will be no more cultural challenges, no more societal struggles, and no more restive relationships.

Everything in the new heaven and new earth will be perfect—perfect joy, perfect peace, perfect love—all blessings from the Father who loved us from the beginning; saved us by the blood of his Son, Jesus; and chose us to be his own through the power of the Spirit. The new heaven and the new earth will be perfect indeed!

Until then, we live our lives torn.

# APPENDIX

*Bible Threads With Dr. Bruce Becker*,
episode 3, season 8, March 27, 2024

"War Zone—A World Full of Evil"

This is the third episode in the podcast series *War Zone*. It's a series in which we're focusing on the devil as he shows up on the pages of the Bible. In this series, we're learning who the devil is, how he operates, and what his tactics and goals are so that *we* can be prepared for his attacks on *us*. To be prepared, we want to **"put on the full armor of God, so that** [we] **can take** [our] **stand against the devil's schemes"** (Ephesians 6:11).

The war zone we are entering into today is described in the first seven verses of Genesis chapter 6. These verses come right before the account of Noah and explain the reason why the Lord God chose to destroy the world through a worldwide flood. In these seven verses, there are three interesting and challenging topics. The first one is a significant literary and theological difficulty involving the phrase "sons of God." The second addresses a group of people known as the Nephilim and what, if any, was their relationship with the sons of God. And the third point informs us what it was and who it was that led God to destroy the world he had created.

Let's start with the first topic. Among Bible scholars, there isn't agreement as to the meaning of these opening verses. The main debate centers around the phrase "sons of God." Who are the sons of God? Well, there are basically two different views as to who the sons of God were, and these two views have nothing in common with each other. So what we're going to do is this: First of all, we'll read these verses, then unpack some of the word meanings and usages, and then dig into the two views as to what Bible scholars claim these verses mean. Now, it seems to me that both views are somewhat plausible, but both also have some challenges. Then to complicate the discussion, we'll look at the Nephilim and ask the question, Are the Nephilim related to the sons of God, or are they unrelated? Just so you know upfront, there are lots of questions in today's episode, some of which will not be answered completely, with only one thing that is absolutely certain. But more on that later.

Genesis 6:1–4 states:

> **When human beings began to increase in number on the earth and daughters were born to them, the sons of God saw that the daughters of humans were beautiful, and they married any of them they chose. Then the Lord said, "My Spirit will not**

**contend with humans forever, for they are mortal; their days will be a hundred and twenty years."**

**The Nephilim were on the earth in those days—and also afterward—when the sons of God went to the daughters of humans and had children by them. They were the heroes of old, men of renown.**

So, the population of the earth was increasing. And the sons of God saw that the daughters of humans were beautiful, and they married any of them they chose. The biblical author seems to draw a stark contrast here between the "sons of God" and the "daughters of humans."

The Hebrew word translated as "married" isn't one of the typical Hebrew words for "marry." The word in this verse simply means "to take." So, literally this verse says that the sons of God took women (plural), any of them they chose. Now the phrase "took women" could refer to marriage. For example, we have an old English phrase that is similar—"to take a wife." But it could also just mean "to take them." Then in verse 4, we learn that the sons of God went to the daughters of humans and had children by them. Whether it was marriage or not, there was a sexual union between the sons of God and the daughters of humans with children being conceived and born.

So, who were the sons of God? Well, first we should examine if this phrase is used anywhere else in the Old Testament. It is. And the phrase refers to two different groups. One way it is used is to refer to the Lord God's chosen people, the descendants of Abraham, Isaac, and Jacob. For example, in the book of Deuteronomy, Moses wrote, **"You are the children of the LORD your God"** (14:1), literally, "You are the sons of the Lord your God." In the book of Jeremiah, the Lord God sought to call his wayward people back to him: **"How gladly would I treat you like my children** [literally 'my sons'] **and give you a pleasant land, the most beautiful inheritance of any nation"** (3:19). Although the Lord God's chosen people are called sons or children, it's not the exact same phrase as we find in Genesis chapter 6. More on this subtle difference in a minute.

The other place the phrase "sons of God" occurs is in the book of Job, three times. In all three cases, the phrase "sons of God" refers to supernatural spirit beings. In the book of Job, most Bible translations translate "sons of God" as "angels," with a footnote that indicates the literal meaning "sons of God." In Job chapter 1, we read, **"One day the angels** [sons of God] **came to present themselves before the LORD, and Satan also came with them"** (verse 6). In the next chapter it says, **"On another day the angels** [sons of God] **came to present themselves before the LORD, and Satan also came with them to present himself before him"** (2:1). Then near the end of the book of Job, the Lord God confronted Job because of his thoughts and words:

> **"Where were you when I laid the earth's foundation? Tell me, if you understand. Who marked off**

> **its dimensions? Surely you know! Who stretched a measuring line across it? On what were its footings set, or who laid its cornerstone—while the morning stars sang together and all the angels** [sons of God] **shouted for joy?"** (38:4–7)

So what's the subtle difference between the two usages of "sons of God"? The phrase used in Genesis chapter 6 is literally "sons of Elohim," Elohim being one of the names for God and translated as "God" in our English Bibles. However, the name for God used in connection with God's covenant people is typically Yahweh, translated into English as "LORD" in small caps. The precise phrase, "sons of Elohim," is never used in the Old Testament to refer to God's covenant people. "Sons of Elohim" is used just five times in the Old Testament, two times in Genesis chapter 6, and three times in the book of Job, where the phrase means supernatural spirit beings.

So, who were the sons of God in Genesis chapter 6? As I mentioned earlier, there are two views among Bible scholars. The first view identifies the sons of God as the godly descendants of Seth who intermarried with the ungodly descendants of Cain. Supporters of this view point to the contrasting genealogies in Genesis chapters 4 and 5. At the end of chapter 4, there is a genealogy of Cain's descendants. In chapter 5, there's a detailed genealogy from Adam to Noah. The main premise with this view is that the descendants of Seth were attracted to the outward beauty of the women descended from Cain and failed to consider the inner beauty of a woman who fears the Lord. The result was that the world became more and more evil with every generation because of this intermarriage. The challenge with this view, however, is that the biblical text states these are sons of God, not descendants of Seth.

The second view is that the sons of God in Genesis chapter 6 like the sons of God described in the book of Job are supernatural spirit beings—namely, rebel angels. Supporters of this view point to the usage of the phrase "sons of God" in the book of Job. It's an example of letting Scripture interpret Scripture. The thought with this view is that the rebel angels saw that the daughters of humans were beautiful, took them, and had children with them. Say what?

How can rebel angels who are spirits engage in sexual activity with human women that results in pregnancy and the birth of babies? That's a fair question. It's a view that seems quite strange to us. But it's no stranger than a snake talking to a woman in the Garden of Eden . . . no stranger than the water of the Red Sea walled up on each side to let the people of Israel cross on dry ground . . . no stranger than the Jordan River being backed up so the people of Israel could cross it into the Promised Land . . . no stranger than a donkey talking to a reluctant prophet . . . no stranger than a big fish swallowing the runaway Jonah. The Bible has plenty of strange accounts. This might be another one. The fact is, we don't always know what goes on in the invisible world of angels and demons.

We do know that angels can take on the form of human beings. We see that in Genesis chapter 18, when three angels came to the home of Abraham and Sarah, one of them being the Lord God himself. The three came to Abraham's home as human beings. To show these men/angels hospitality:

> **Abraham hurried into the tent to Sarah. "Quick," he said, "get three seahs of the finest flour and knead it and bake some bread."**
>
> **Then he ran to the herd and selected a choice, tender calf and gave it to a servant, who hurried to prepare it. He then brought some curds and milk and the calf that had been prepared, and set these before them. While they ate, he stood near them under a tree.** (verses 6–8)

So here we have angels eating food as humans do.

Two of the men, later identified as angels, left Abraham and Sarah's home and headed toward Sodom and Gomorrah, two cities near the Dead Sea. The angel of the Lord, God himself, stayed and informed Abraham that he was about to destroy the two cities because of their wickedness. When the two angels arrived at Sodom, Lot, who was Abraham's nephew, urged the two men to stay the night in his home. But **"before they had gone to bed, all the men from every part of the city of Sodom—both young and**

**old—surrounded the house. They called to Lot, "Where are the men who came to you tonight? Bring them out to us so that we can have sex with them"** (Genesis 19:4,5). The men of Sodom didn't know that the two men in Lot's house were angels. They thought they were men with whom they could have gay sex.

So if the sons of God in Genesis chapter 6 were rebel angels, then in reality they masqueraded as human males and had illicit sexual union with human women during the days leading up to Noah and the flood. It still sounds strange to us, doesn't it? So I bet you're wondering if the Bible gives us any further insight into this. It does. Let's go to the New Testament and take a look at the two letters written by the apostle Peter and the brief letter written by Jude.

In chapter 3 of his first letter, the apostle Peter wrote about the events of Good Friday through Easter Sunday:

> **For Christ also suffered once for sins, the righteous for the unrighteous, to bring you to God. He was put to death in the body but made alive in the Spirit. After being made alive, he went and made proclamation to the imprisoned spirits—to those who were disobedient long ago when God waited patiently in the days of Noah while the ark was being built.** (verses 18-20)

After Jesus rose from the dead, he went and made a proclamation of his victory over sin, death, and the devil to the spirits in prison. These spirits in prison had been disobedient when? . . . during the days of Noah. And there's more.

In Peter's second letter, he wrote to God's people about how God rescues the righteous. He also wrote about how God punishes the wicked:

> **For if God did not spare angels when they sinned, but sent them to hell, putting them in chains of darkness to be held for judgment; if he did not spare the ancient world when he brought the flood on its ungodly people, but protected Noah, a preacher of righteousness, and seven others; if he condemned the cities of Sodom and Gomorrah by burning them to ashes, and made them an example of what is going to happen to the ungodly . . .** (2:4–7)

Following this, Peter mentioned how God rescued Lot, a man who is called righteous.

Here Peter cited three Old Testament events to demonstrate how God punished the wicked. Let's take them in reverse order. The third event Peter cited was the destruction of Sodom and Gomorrah. That event is recorded in Genesis chapter 19. The second event he cited was the flood, which destroyed the world except for eight people. That event is found in the last part of Genesis chapter 6 and continues through chapter 8. The first event that Peter cited involved the sinning of angels in the days of Noah. As a result of their sin, God put them in chains until the judgment.

This sounds much like what Peter wrote in his first letter, where spirits were in prison for disobeying the Lord in the days of Noah. Then, in verses 9 and 10, Peter contrasted the rescue of the righteous and the punishment of the wicked: **"If this is so, then the Lord knows how to rescue the godly from trials and to hold the unrighteous for punishment on the day of judgment. This is especially true of those who follow the *corrupt desire of the flesh* and *despise authority*** (2 Peter 2:9,10, emphasis added). So, is this first event that Peter wrote about angels sinning what we find in the first four verses of Genesis chapter 6? Just think about that for a moment. There's more.

Let's turn to Jude's letter. Jude wrote: **"And the angels who did not keep their positions of authority but abandoned their proper dwelling—these he has kept in darkness, bound with everlasting chains for judgment on the great Day. In a similar way, Sodom and Gomorrah and the surrounding towns gave themselves up to sexual immorality and perversion. They serve as an example of those who suffer the punishment of eternal fire"** (Jude 1:6,7).

Like Peter, Jude addressed the sin of the rebel angels. He described it as these angels not keeping their positions of authority and abandoning their dwelling place. Peter mentioned that God kept them in darkness and kept them chained until the judgment. And then he made a comparison to Sodom and Gomorrah. He compared the sexual immorality and perversion of the people of Sodom and Gomorrah to the rebel angels. "In a similar way," he wrote. In a similar way to the sexual immorality and perversion of Sodom and Gomorrah were the rebel angels who didn't keep their positions of authority and abandoned their dwelling place. The phrase "in a similar way" is key to understanding what the rebel angels were guilty of and why they were chained until the final judgment.

We should probably address what is meant by these rebel angels being chained. It doesn't seem to mean that they were physically chained, because they're spirits, but that they were prevented from doing what they had previously done.

So, there you have the two views of who the sons of God were. Either God-fearing sons of Seth or rebel angels. And as I said earlier, there is not agreement among Bible scholars. I may be wrong, but taking into account what "sons of God" means in the book of Job and what Peter and Jude wrote in their letters, it seems to me that the sons of God in Genesis chapter 6 being rebel angels is the most plausible. But feel free to disagree.

Let's discuss another topic on which there isn't agreement. Are the Nephilim related to the sons of God or are they unrelated? In Genesis 6:4, we read, **"The Nephilim were on the earth in those days—and also afterward—when the sons of God went to the daughters of humans and had children by them. They were the heroes of old, men of renown."** The word "Nephilim" is a plural Hebrew word that means "giants." One view of the Nephilim is that they were the offspring of the sons of God and the daughters of humans. This view seems plausible except for the fact that the biblical text indicates that they existed before the flood *and* after the flood. All but eight people died in the Genesis flood, including the offspring of the sons of God and daughters of humans.

The other view of who the Nephilim were was that these were exceptionally large and strong mighty men. Somewhere in the genetic code of Adam and Eve there were genes that produced mighty men. Which also meant that somewhere in the genetic code of Noah and his wife there remained genes that produced mighty men. Think of Goliath, for example.

There is one other place in the Old Testament that mentions the Nephilim. It is when Moses sent spies into the land of Canaan and 10 of the 12 men reported back:

> **"We can't attack those people; they are stronger than we are." And they spread among the Israelites a bad report about the land they had explored. They said, "The land we explored devours those living in it. All the people we saw there are of great size. We saw the Nephilim there (the descendants of Anak come from the Nephilim). We seemed like grasshoppers in our own eyes, and we looked the same to them."** (Numbers 13:31–33)

So the fact that the Nephilim existed after the flood suggests that they weren't the offspring of the sons of God and the daughters of men.

There may be uncertainty as to who the sons of God were. There may be uncertainty as to who the Nephilim were. But in Genesis chapter 6, there is no uncertainty as to why God destroyed the world through a worldwide flood:

> **The Lord saw how great the wickedness of the human race had become on the earth, and that every inclination of the thoughts of the human heart was only evil all the time. The Lord regretted that he had made human beings on the earth, and his heart was deeply troubled. So the Lord said, "I will wipe from the face of the earth the human race I have created—and with them the animals, the birds and the creatures that move along the ground—for I regret that I have made them."** (verses 5-7)

At the time of Noah, this earth was a world full of evil. Think about it. Every inclination of the thoughts of the human heart was only evil all the time. Do you ever think the world in which we live is headed in that direction, only evil all the time? Some days it seems that way. Although the source of evil is not mentioned in this section of God's Word, we know who was behind it—the devil, Satan. He is the evil one.

When the disciples asked Jesus how they should pray, Jesus included in his prayer a petition that addressed the evil one: **"And lead us not into temptation, but deliver us from the evil one"** (Matthew 6:13). The apostle Paul, in his letter to the Christians living in Ephesus, wrote:

> **Finally, be strong in the Lord and in his mighty power. Put on the full armor of God, so that you can take your stand against the devil's schemes. For our struggle is not against flesh and blood, but against the rulers, against the authorities, against the powers of this dark world and against the spiritual forces of evil in the heavenly realms. Therefore put on the full armor of God, so that when the day of evil comes, you may be able to stand your ground, and after you have done everything, to stand. Stand firm then, with the belt of truth buckled around your waist, with the breastplate of righteousness in place, and with your feet fitted with the readiness that comes from the gospel of peace. In addition to all this, take up the shield of faith, with which you can extinguish all the flaming arrows of the evil one.** (6:10–16)

The one thing certain from Genesis chapter 6 is that the world was full of evil and the evil one was behind it. The evil one still is working in our world today. The only way to fight against him and defeat him is to put on the full armor of God.

# NOTES

1. Johannes P. Louw and Eugene Albert Nida, eds., *Greek-English Lexicon of the New Testament: Based on Semantic Domains* (New York: United Bible Societies, 1996), 351.

2. Thomas Rawson Taylor, 1807–35, "I'm But a Stranger Here," text is public domain.

3. *2024 Trafficking in Persons Report*, "Global Law Enforcement Data" and "Regional Maps," U.S. Department of State, accessed October 24, 2024, https://www.state.gov/reports/2024-trafficking-in-persons-report/.

4. "Global Slavery Index: Global Findings," Walk Free, accessed October 24, 2024, https://www.walkfree.org/global-slavery-index/findings/global-findings/#:~:text=An%20estimated%2050%20million%20people,million%20were%20in%20forced%20marriages.

5. *Merriam-Webster Online*, s.v. "genecide," accessed October 16, 2024, https://www.merriam-webster.com/dictionary/genocide.

6. Ronald Reagan, "January 5, 1967: Inaugural Address (Public Ceremony)," Ronald Reagan Presidential Library

& Museum, accessed October 24, 2024, https://www.reaganlibrary.gov/archives/speech/january-5-1967-inaugural-address-public-ceremony.

7. "Nero Persecutes the Christians, 64 A.D.," EyeWitness to History.com, accessed October 25, 2024, http://www.eyewitnesstohistory.com/christians.htm.

8. "#103: Polycarp's Martyrdom," Christian History Institute, accessed October 25, 2025, https://christianhistoryinstitute.org/study/module/polycarp.

9. Everett Ferguson, "Persecution in the Early Church: Did You Know?" *Christianity Today*, accessed October 25, 2024, https://www.christianitytoday.com/history/issues/issue-27/persecution-in-early-church-did-you-know.html.

10. "World Watch List 2024," Open Doors, accessed October 25, 2024, https://www.opendoors.org/en-US/persecution/countries/.

11. Mark A. Jeske, *James; 1,2 Peter; 1,2,3 John; Jude* of The People's Bible series (Milwaukee: Northwestern Publishing House, 2002), 114–115.

12. Ibid., 169–171.

# ABOUT THE AUTHOR

**Dr. Bruce Becker** currently serves as the executive vice president for Time of Grace. He is a respected and well-known author, award-winning podcaster, and public speaker. He has served as the lead pastor of two congregations; as a member of several boards; and on many commissions, committees, and task forces. In 2012 he completed his professional doctorate in leadership and ministry management. Bruce and his wife, Linda, live in Jackson, Wisconsin.

Find his podcast, *Bible Threads With Dr. Bruce Becker*, at timeofgrace.org, Apple Podcasts, Spotify, and many other podcasting platforms or by scanning this code:

# OTHER BOOKS BY BRUCE

*True Crimes of the Bible*

*More Tough Questions*

*Gifted for More*

FIND THESE BOOKS AND MORE BY SCANNING THE CODE OR VISITING TIMEOFGRACE.STORE.

# ABOUT TIME OF GRACE

The mission of Time of Grace is to point people to what matters most: Jesus. Using a variety of media (television, radio, podcasts, print publications, and digital), Time of Grace teaches tough topics in an approachable and relatable way, accessible in multiple languages, making the Bible clear and understandable for those who need encouragement in their walks of faith and for those who don't yet know Jesus at all.

TO DISCOVER MORE,
PLEASE VISIT TIMEOFGRACE.ORG
OR SCAN THIS CODE:

# HELP SHARE GOD'S MESSAGE OF GRACE!

Every gift you give helps Time of Grace reach people around the world with the good news of Jesus. Your generosity and prayer support take the gospel of grace to others through our ministry outreach and help them experience a satisfied life as they see God all around them.

GIVE TODAY AT
TIMEOFGRACE.ORG/GIVE,
BY CALLING 800.661.3311, OR BY
SCANNING THE CODE BELOW.

THANK YOU!